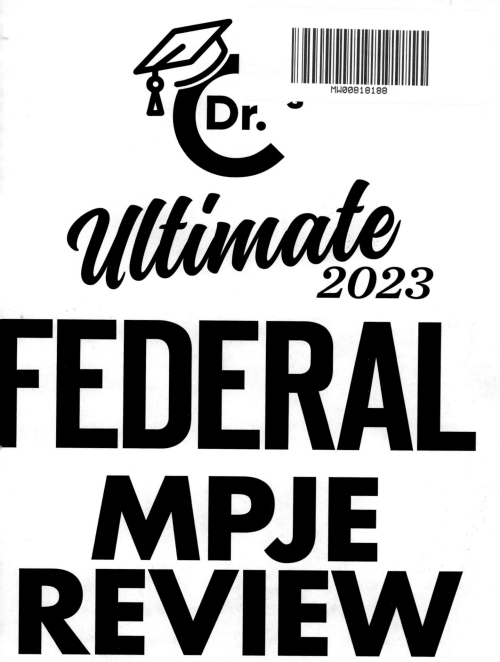

Dr. C

Ultimate *2023*

FEDERAL MPJE REVIEW

MASTERING THE MPJE COMPETENCIES

GARY CACCIATORE, Pharm.D., J.D.

Published by Dr. C's Review Guides
Updates and corrections available at http://www.mpjereviews.com
info@mpjereviews.com

February 2023

ISBN 979-8-218-08987-0

CONTENTS

INTRODUCTION

The Multistate Pharmacy Jurisprudence Exam (MPJE[1]) is used by most states as part of the licensure requirements for pharmacists. Whether you are a graduating pharmacy student or a seasoned pharmacist trying to get licensed in another state, the exam can be difficult. Data from the National Association of Boards of Pharmacy (NABP) indicate that for 2021 the average passing rate for all test takers of the MPJE from all accredited pharmacy schools was 83.45%.[2] This is lower than the passing rate for the North American Pharmacist Licensure Exam (NAPLEX[3]). Several schools have good passing rates on the NAPLEX but struggle obtaining the same results with the MPJE. Part of the difficulty of the MPJE is that pharmacists and pharmacy students may have good general knowledge of the legal requirements to practice but do not appreciate the level of detail required to perform well on the MPJE. Because the MPJE covers both federal and state law, adequate preparation requires reviewing both. This book provides an overview of the MPJE and a review of the federal laws and rules with study tips to help the reader prepare for the MPJE in any state. The material must be supplemented with applicable state laws in order to be adequately prepared.

Chapter 1 of this book takes the unique approach of analyzing and explaining the MPJE competency statements to help the reader understand what topics are likely to be tested. Chapters 2 and 3 focus on the primary areas of federal law that are covered on the MPJE. Chapter 4 is written by one of the country's leading experts on United States Pharmacopeia (USP) standards applicable to pharmacy, Patricia Kienle, R.Ph., MPA, BCSCP, FASHP, who provides an excellent summary of the USP chapters 795, 797, and 800. Finally, Chapter 5 includes self-assessment questions with explanatory answers on the federal law topics covered in the book.

My goal in developing this book was to apply many of the study tips and legal teaching techniques that I have used in my successful review guides for Texas, Florida, and Pennsylvania to the MPJE in general. I hope

---

1. MPJE is a registered trademark of the National Association of Boards of Pharmacy.
2. Multistate Pharmacy Jurisprudence Examination Passing Rates for 2019–2021 Graduates Per Pharmacy School.
3. NAPLEX is a registered trademark of the National Association of Boards of Pharmacy.

you find this to be a helpful resource as you develop your study plan for the MPJE. For more MPJE resources go to mpjereviews.com.

I would like to thank Patricia Kienle for her expertise and authorship of Chapter 4 and Kurt Wehrs and Motto Publishing Services for their dedicated assistance in helping me make this publication a reality.

ABOUT THE AUTHOR

Gary Cacciatore, Pharm.D., J.D.

Gary Cacciatore is the founder and President of Dr. C's Review Guides. In 2021, he retired from Cardinal Health, where he served as Associate Regulatory Counsel and Vice President of Regulatory Affairs.

Prior to joining Cardinal Health, Dr. Cacciatore was an Assistant Professor at the University of Houston College of Pharmacy and the University of Houston Law Center, where he taught courses in pharmacy law and ethics, drug information, and food and drug law. He currently serves as an Adjunct Associate Professor at the University of Houston College of Pharmacy and as an Adjunct Associate Professor at the University of Florida College of Pharmacy.

Dr. Cacciatore has taught pharmacy law full-time or part-time for over 25 years and is the co-author of *Texas and Federal Pharmacy and Drug Law*, a comprehensive textbook used by nearly all of the pharmacy schools in Texas. He is also the author of state-specific MPJE reviews for Texas, Florida, and Pennsylvania. Dr. C's MPJE review guides have been utilized by over 25,000 candidates in all 50 states and in 14 countries.

Dr. Cacciatore received his Doctor of Pharmacy degree with high honors from the University of Florida College of Pharmacy. He earned his Doctor of Jurisprudence degree with honors from the University of Houston Law Center. He is a past President of the American Society for Pharmacy Law (ASPL) and in 2015 received the Joseph L. Fink III Founders Award from ASPL for outstanding and sustained contributions to the professions of pharmacy and law. Dr. Cacciatore was named the Outstanding Alumnus by the University of Florida College of Pharmacy for 2021.

Dr. Cacciatore is admitted to the bar in Texas and is a registered pharmacist in Texas and Florida.

ACRONYMS

Most acronyms are defined the first time they are used in this book (and often several times), but here is a list of some of the major acronyms used:

ACPE	Accreditation Council for Pharmacy Education
APRN	Advanced Practice Registered Nurse
CE	Continuing Education
CEU	Continuing Education Unit
CFR	Code of Federal Regulations
cGMP	Current Good Manufacturing Practices
DEA	Drug Enforcement Administration
FCSA	Federal Controlled Substances Act
FDA	Food and Drug Administration
FDCA	Food, Drug, and Cosmetic Act (Federal)
HIPAA	Health Insurance Portability and Accountability Act
LTCF	Long Term Care Facility
MPJE	Multistate Pharmacy Jurisprudence Exam
NABP	National Association of Boards of Pharmacy
NAPLEX	North American Pharmacist Licensure Exam
NDC	National Drug Code
OTC	Over-the-Counter
PA	Physician Assistant
PIC	Pharmacist-in-Charge
PMP	Prescription Monitoring Program
PPI	Patient Package Insert
PPPA	Poison Prevention Packaging Act
REMS	Risk Evaluation and Mitigation Strategies
USP	United States Pharmacopeia

OVERVIEW OF THE MULTISTATE PHARMACY JURISPRUDENCE EXAM

Registration Bulletin

Detailed information on the MPJE is available from the National Association of Boards of Pharmacy (NABP) website at www.nabp.pharmacy as well as in the NAPLEX/MPJE Candidate Application Bulletin, which is available for download on the website. The bulletin contains detailed information on registering for the exam, scheduling testing appointments, fees, identification requirements, security, question types, and exam results. Candidates should download and read the Candidate Application Bulletin carefully as well as visit the NABP website for additional information specific to the MPJE.

Exam Content and Structure

The MPJE is a 120-item computer-based examination that uses adaptive technology. This means the computer adapts the questions you receive based on your previous responses. You must complete 107 questions for your exam to be scored. Of the 120 items on the exam, 100 count toward your score. The questions not counting toward your score are being pretested; however, you will not know which questions count toward your score and which questions are being pretested. You are allowed 2½ hours to complete the exam. Because it is a computer-based examination, you cannot go back and review a question or change an answer once you have confirmed it and moved to the next question. You also cannot skip a question. Since there is a penalty for unanswered questions, you should answer all the questions.

The exam content and questions are developed by Board of Pharmacy representatives, practitioners, and educators from around the country who serve as item writers. Each state board of pharmacy approves the questions that are used for its state.

Previously, results were reported on a scaled score, and candidates had to achieve a score of 75 to pass the exam. This is not 75% but a scaled score whereby your performance is measured against predetermined minimum abilities. NABP no longer reports actual scores. Scores are only reported as pass or fail, and results are generally provided seven business days after you take the exam. Candidates are allowed five attempts to pass the exam.

While you must have a good base knowledge of the laws and rules governing the practice of pharmacy in your state, simply memorizing the laws will not suffice. The exam is not simply questions that ask you to identify or repeat the law. There are many situational questions that will require you to apply the law to the facts provided. These types of questions are not as easy. When approaching these types of questions, it is helpful to remember that the goal of the boards of pharmacy is to protect the public health. Answers that address that goal are most likely to be correct. At the same time, the boards of pharmacy also must enforce the laws, so many of the laws and rules are intended to assist the board with that function. Rules related to recordkeeping and documentation are especially important to the boards of pharmacy to help them identify who or what caused an error in a pharmacy that may cause patient harm. Keeping these functions of the boards of pharmacy in mind may help you in trying to choose between answers on the exam.

The MPJE consists of several types of questions, including multiple choice, multiple response, and ordered response. Examples of each question type are provided below:

Multiple Choice Sample Question

If authorized by the prescriber, what is the maximum number of times a prescription for tramadol may be refilled?

a. 2 times
b. 3 times
c. 5 times
d. 0 times (tramadol prescriptions may not be refilled)

Multiple Response Sample Question

Which of the following disclosures of protected health information may be made without written consent from the patient? **Select all that apply.**

_____ Sending a patient's prescription information to an insurance company for payment purposes
_____ Providing a list of a patient's prescription information to the patient's primary care physician
_____ Reporting controlled substance prescription information to the prescription monitoring program
_____ Sending a list of a patient's prescription information to a drug manufacturer

> **STUDY TIP:** When answering multiple response questions, it is recommended that you choose more than one answer. If only one answer is correct, it is more likely to be a multiple choice question.

Ordered Response Sample Question

Place the following products in order from the least abuse potential to the greatest abuse potential. (All options must be used.) Left-click the mouse to highlight, drag, and order the answer options.

Unordered Options	Ordered Response
Tylenol with Codeine #3	_____
Sudafed	_____
Valium	_____
Vicodin	_____

> **STUDY TIP:** Make sure you read the ordered response question carefully and put the items in the correct order and not the reverse order. Double-check the order before hitting the submit button.

Federal versus State Law

When comparing federal law versus state law, the general rule is you always follow the stricter law. In the rare instance where state and federal law directly conflict so that you cannot follow one without violating the other, the federal law would prevail. It is important to understand that no distinction is made on the MPJE exam between federal and state law questions. You should answer each question in terms of the prevailing laws of the state in which you are seeking licensure.

> **STUDY TIP:** You should not see a question on the exam that starts out with the words, "According to the Federal Controlled Substances Act . . ." Such a question would not be valid because it is asking you to answer the question based on federal law only. If a state law is different and stricter than the federal law, that is the law that must be followed and would be the correct answer.

This book only covers federal law, and while many states follow the federal law in some areas, there are several topics where state law will be stricter than the federal law. Many of the competency statements for the MPJE are only addressed in state law. I have indicated those areas and noted where it is particularly important to consult your state law in Chapter 1.

Practice Questions and Pre-MPJE

This book provides self-assessment questions to help you assess your comprehension of the material, but these questions are based only on the federal laws and rules or USP Chapters. These questions can be helpful in areas where the law is the same in a state, but because of the variability of state laws, you should also use practice questions that are targeted to the state in which you plan to take the MPJE. There are several sources of state practice questions available, but I have not reviewed them all, so I cannot make a recommendation on which one to use. Just realize that if a practice question you come across is based only on federal law, the correct answer could be incorrect in your state. Also, the laws and rules are always changing, so it is possible that practice questions you come across may not have been updated with the latest information. There is only one source of MPJE practice questions that provides you with actual MPJE questions from previous exams that are no longer used, and that is the Pre-MPJE exam offered by NABP. Candidates can register to take the Pre-MPJE online at NABP's website. The exam consists of 40 questions, and 50 minutes are allotted to complete the exam. The Pre-MPJE can be taken only one time for each jurisdiction a person is seeking licensure in.

There are other websites using the term "Pre-MPJE" that are not affiliated with NABP.

Basic Study and Preparation Tips

Below are helpful study and preparation tips to consider for the MPJE:

- Read and review relevant laws, regulations, and available government resources.
- Revisit pharmacy law course materials from pharmacy school (if recent graduate) and update any information that is outdated.
- When completing any practice questions, make sure you understand the concept and why the correct answer is correct and the other options are incorrect.
- Make and memorize charts and lists (e.g., label requirements, quantities, time frames).
- Be prepared to read exam directions and questions carefully and recall applicable laws.
- Be prepared to apply knowledge and skills of relevant laws and regulations.
- Be prepared to select the best answer. Do not overanalyze the questions or focus on the very rare instances that may change the answer.
- Be prepared to use time management skills during the exam (approximately 1.25 minutes per question).
- Do not rely on what your own work environment does. Your employer may have additional or stricter policies, but you must answer exam questions based on the legal and regulatory requirements.
- Do not overlook important words such as "must," "can," "should," and "may."
- Do not forget to consider federal and state laws, choosing the stricter requirement when both apply.
- Do your best to remain relaxed and focused.

MPJE Competency Statements

Each question on the MPJE is tied to a specific competency statement. You must master a certain number of competencies to pass the exam. Do not panic if you receive more than one question on the exam that is on the same topic or even one similar to a previous question. Do not assume you missed a previous question and need to change your answer on the next question that is similar. While it is certainly true that you could have answered a question incorrectly on a particular competency statement, sometimes you have to answer more than one question correctly in order to pass a particular competency, depending on the difficulty of the questions. In addition, you may receive a similar question or questions from the same competency because one or more of those questions are being pre-tested and do not count toward your score.

It is important that you are familiar with the competency statements in the registration bulletin. Chapter 1 of this book goes through each of the MPJE competency statements with detailed explanations for each one, providing guidance on what to study and what to look for in state laws to master each competency.

CHAPTER ONE
Mastering the MPJE Competencies

CHAPTER ONE
Mastering the MPJE Competencies

This chapter will review the MPJE competency statements in detail and explain what I believe each competency statement is expecting you to know. To be clear, I have no knowledge of the actual questions that are on the MPJE, but I have found that students and pharmacists preparing for the MPJE sometimes misinterpret the competency statements and end up studying material that is not applicable.

New MPJE competency statements became effective January 1, 2023. The new competencies are much broader statements than previous versions. This makes it more difficult to determine the topics that may be covered on the exam. The previous version of the competency statements did need to be revised as they were a bit unorganized and repetitive. However, one advantage they did provide was that they gave better insight into the topics that may be covered on the exam because they were more specific. Because of this, I have included a cross-reference chart that includes the new competency statements as well as some of the previous competency statements that may be included as part of the new competency. I also include discussions of those topics throughout the chapter as it is likely that many of those same topics are still covered on the exam. The explanations and study tips provided are based on my best guess of what the expectations are for these competency statements, but I may not cover every topic they will expect you to know. Finally, the tremendous variability of state laws means I cannot address every item that may be covered under a particular competency statement, but I have pointed out the federal laws that address the competency statements, and those topics are covered in detail in the other chapters. I have indicated those competencies that are based only on state law, and for many of those areas I have provided suggestions on what to focus on in reviewing your state laws and rules.

It is important to understand that not all the competencies will apply in each jurisdiction. If there is no federal law or rule that addresses a competency and it is not addressed in your state laws or rules, it is unlikely that a question on that competency would appear on the MPJE for your state. However, sometimes the competency is addressing a topic that is addressed in state law, but the laws or rules in a state may use different terminology. Thus, simply searching for the terms found in the competency statements in the state laws and rules is not a comprehensive study strategy. I have identified some of those situations where laws and terminology vary from state to state, but it is impossible to address all the terms that may be used in every state. What is important is that you understand the intent of the competency statements and ensure that you identify if and where that topic is addressed in the jurisdiction for which you are taking the exam.

MPJE
Competency Statements
Cross Reference Chart

This chart lists the 2023 MPJE Competency Statements in the left column and related previous competency statements in the right column. This is an attempt to provide more detail to the new competency statements to help candidates understand the topics that may be covered.

Disclaimer: The author was not involved in drafting the new competency statements and there is no guarantee that this chart is completely accurate or that all the previous competency statements are included. Some previous statements may have been purposely eliminated or may be incorporated into multiple sections. Previous competency statements that did not seem to fit within any of the new competency statements are not included. This chart is not approved by or endorsed by NABP.

2023 MPJE Competency Statements	Related Previous MPJE Competency Statements
Area 1: Licensure/Personnel (approximately 22% of the exam)	
1.1 Responsibilities of the pharmacist and non-pharmacist personnel: • 1.1.1 Qualifications, scope of duties, limitations and restrictions of duties, or conditions to practice for pharmacists-in-charge (or equivalent) and pharmacists • 1.1.2 Qualifications, scope of duties, limitations, and restrictions of duties, or conditions to practice for non-pharmacist personnel	1.1 Legal Responsibilities of the pharmacist and other pharmacy personnel • 1.1.1 Unique legal responsibilities of the pharmacist-in-charge (or equivalent), pharmacists, interns, and pharmacy owners • 1.1.2 Qualifications, scope of duties, and conditions for practice relating to pharmacy technicians and all other non-pharmacist personnel Personnel ratios, duties, tasks, roles, and functions of non-pharmacist personnel
1.2 Licensures, registrations, and certifications for pharmacists or non-pharmacist personnel: • 1.2.1 Qualifications, examinations, internships, maintaining pharmacist competency, and renewals of licensures, registrations, or certifications	2.1 Qualifications, application procedure, necessary examinations, and internship for licensure, registration, or certification of individuals engaged in the storage, distribution, and/or dispensing of pharmaceutical products (prescription and nonprescription) *(continued)*

5
Copyright © 2023 Gary Cacciatore

2023 MPJE Competency Statements	Related Previous MPJE Competency Statements
Area 1: Licensure/Personnel (approximately 22% of the exam)	

(*continued*)
• 1.2.2 Classifications and processes of disciplinary actions
• 1.2.3 Reporting to and participating in programs addressing the inability to practice with reasonable skill and safety
	• 2.1.1 Requirements for special or restricted licenses, registration, authorization, or certificates
	    Pharmacists, pharmacist preceptors, pharmacy interns, pharmacy technicians, controlled substance registrants, and under specialty pharmacist licenses (Nuclear, Consultant, etc.)
	• 2.1.2 . . . maintaining competency
	• 2.1.3 Requirements for classifications and processes of disciplinary actions that may be taken against a registered, licensed, certified, or permitted individual
	• 2.1.4 Requirements for the reporting to and participating in programs addressing the inability of an individual licensed, registered, or certified by the Board to engage in the practice of pharmacy with reasonable skill and safety
	    Impairment caused by the use of alcohol, drugs, chemicals, or other materials, or mental, physical, or psychological conditions

Area 2: Pharmacist Practice (approximately 33% of the exam)	
2.1 Requirements for issuing prescriptions/drug orders: • 2.1.1 Requirements for drug uses, limitations, or restrictions • 2.1.2 Scope of authority, scope of practice, limitations or restrictions of practice, and valid registration of practitioners who are authorized to prescribe, dispense, or administer drugs • 2.1.3 Requirements for issuing non-controlled prescriptions/drug orders • 2.1.4 Requirements for issuing controlled prescriptions/drug orders	1.3 Legal requirements that must be observed in the issuance of a prescription/drug order • 1.3.1 Prescription/order requirements for pharmaceutical products and the limitations on their respective therapeutic uses Products, preparations, their uses, and limitations applicable to all prescribed orders for both human and veterinary uses • 1.3.2 Scope of authority, scope of practice, and valid registration of all practitioners who are autho-

2023 MPJE Competency Statements	Related Previous MPJE Competency Statements
Area 2: Pharmacist Practice (approximately 33% of the exam)	

(continued)
• 2.1.5 Authority limitations of practitioners' ability to authorize refills
	rized under law to prescribe, dispense, or administer pharmaceutical products, including controlled substances
	    Federal and state registrations, methadone programs, office-based opioid treatment programs, regulations related to retired or deceased prescribers, internet prescribing, and limits on jurisdictional prescribing
	• 1.3.4 Requirements for issuing a prescription/order.
	    Content and format for written, telephonic voice transmission, electronic facsimile, computer, and internet, during emergency conditions, and tamper-evident prescription forms
	• 1.3.5 Requirements for the issuance of controlled substance prescriptions/orders
	    Content and format for written, telephonic voice transmission, electronic facsimile, computer, and internet, during emergency conditions for changing a prescription, time limits for dispensing initial prescriptions/drug orders, and requirements for multiple Schedule II orders

2.2 Conditions under which the pharmacist or non-pharmacist personnel participates in the administration of drugs or in the management of patients' therapy	1.3.3 Conditions under which the pharmacist participates in the administration of pharmaceutical products or in the management of patients; drug therapy Prescriptive authority, collaborative practice, consulting, counseling, medication administration (including immunizations and vaccines), ordering labs, medication therapy management, and disease state management

(continued)

2023 MPJE Competency Statements	Related Previous MPJE Competency Statements
Area 2: Pharmacist Practice (approximately 33% of the exam) (*continued*)	
2.3 Requirements regarding counseling: • 2.3.1 Counseling or offering to counsel • 2.3.2 Documenting counseling or documenting offering to counsel	1.5 Conditions for making an offer to counsel or counseling appropriate patients including the requirements for documentation • 1.5.1 Requirements to counsel or make an offer to counsel • 1.5.2 Required documentation necessary for counseling
2.4 Returning or reusing drugs	1.4.11 Conditions regarding the return and/or reuse of pharmaceutical products, preparations, bulk drug substances/excipients, and devices Charitable programs, cancer or other repository programs, previously dispensed, and from "will call" areas of pharmacies
2.5 Regulations and agencies regarding pharmacy practice: • 2.5.1 Requirements for promoting quality and safety of public health • 2.5.2 Protecting patient and health record confidentiality	*Note: There is not a specific competency that matches the new 2.5.1, but it is such a broad statement that it likely incorporates any FDA or Board of Pharmacy rule. The closest old competency may be 3.1 which has always been a "catch-all" category.* 3.1. Application of regulations 3.1.1 Laws and rules that regulate or affect the manufacture, storage, distribution, and dispensing of pharmaceutical products, preparations, bulk drug substances/excipients, and devices (prescription and nonprescription), including controlled substances Food, Drug, and Cosmetic Act(s) and Regulations, the Controlled Substances Act(s) and Regulations, OBRA 90's Title IV Requirements, Practice Acts and Rules, other statutes, and regulations, including but not limited to dispensing methadone, child-resistant packaging, tamper-resistant packaging, drug paraphernalia, drug samples, pharmacist responsibilities in Medicare-certified skilled nursing facilities, NDC numbers, and schedules of controlled substances.

2023 MPJE Competency Statements	Related Previous MPJE Competency Statements
Area 2: Pharmacist Practice (approximately 33% of the exam)	
(continued)	1.7.3 Requirements for protecting patient confidentiality and confidential health records HIPAA requirements and conditions for access and use of information
Area 3: Dispensing Requirements (approximately 24% of the exam)	
3.1 Responsibilities for determining whether prescriptions/drug orders are issued for a legitimate medical purpose and within all applicable restrictions	1.4.1 Responsibilities for determining whether prescriptions/orders were issued for a legitimate medical purpose and within all applicable legal restrictions Corresponding responsibility, maximum quantities, restricted distribution systems, red flags/automated alerts, controlled substances, valid patient/prescriber relationship, and due diligence to ensure validity of the order
3.2 Transferring prescription/drug order information between pharmacies by authorized personnel	1.4.2 Requirements for the transfer of existing prescription/order information from one pharmacist to another
3.3 Prospective drug utilization reviews: • 3.3.1 Requirements for reporting to PMP and accessing PMP data	1.4.4 Conditions under which prospective drug use review is conducted prior to dispensing Patient-specific therapy and requirements for patient-specific documentation 1.4.14 Requirements for reporting to PMP, accessing information in a PMP, and the maintenance of security and confidentiality of information accessed in PMPs
3.4 Exceptions to dispensing or refilling prescriptions/drug orders	1.4.3 Conditions under which a prescription/order may be filled or refilled Emergency fills or refills, partial dispensing of a controlled substance, disaster or emergency protocol, patient identification, requirement for death with dignity, medical marijuana, and conscience/moral circumstances *Note: It is unclear if these items fall under the new 3.4, but they are important concepts that may still be on the exam.*

(continued)

2023 MPJE Competency Statements	Related Previous MPJE Competency Statements
Area 3: Dispensing Requirements (approximately 24% of the exam) (*continued*)	
3.5 Labeling of dispensed drugs	1.4.6 Requirements for the labeling of pharmaceutical products and preparations dispensed pursuant to a prescription/order
3.6 Packaging of dispensed drugs	1.4.7 Packaging requirements of pharmaceutical products, preparations, and devices to be dispensed pursuant to a prescription/order Child-resistant and customized medication packaging
3.7 Drug product conditions prohibiting dispensing	1.4.8 Conditions under which a pharmaceutical product, preparation, or device may not be dispensed Adulteration, misbranding, and dating
3.8 Requirements for the distribution and/or dispensing of non-prescription pharmaceutical products, including controlled substances and hazardous drugs: • 3.8.1 Dispensing or administration • 3.8.2 Labeling of non-prescription drugs and devices • 3.8.3 Packaging and repackaging of non-prescription drugs and behind-the-counter products • 3.8.4 Dispensing restricted, non-prescription drugs	1.6 Requirements for the distribution and/or dispensing of non-prescription pharmaceutical products including controlled substances • 1.6.1 Requirements for the labeling of nonprescription pharmaceutical products and devices • 1.6.2 Requirements for the packaging and repackaging of nonprescription pharmaceutical products and devices • 1.6.3 Requirements for the distribution and/or dispensing of poisons, restricted, non-prescription pharmaceutical products, and other restricted materials or devices Pseudoephedrine, dextromethorphan, emergency contraception, and behind-the-counter products as appropriate
Area 4: Pharmacy Operations (approximately 21% of the exam)	
4.1 Ordering, acquisition, and distribution of drugs, including maintenance and content of such records: • 4.1.1 Ordering and acquisition, including the maintenance and content of such records • 4.1.2 Distribution, including the maintenance and content of such records	1.2 Requirements for the acquisition and distribution of pharmaceutical products, including samples • 1.2.1 Requirements and record-keeping in relation to the ordering, acquiring, and maintenance of all pharmaceutical products and bulk drug substances/excipients

2023 MPJE Competency Statements	Related Previous MPJE Competency Statements
Area 4: Pharmacy Operations (approximately 21% of the exam)	
(continued)	Legitimate suppliers, pedigrees, and the maintenance of acquisition records • 1.2.2 Requirements for distributing pharmaceutical products and preparations, including the content and maintenance of distribution records Legal possession of pharmaceutical products (including drug samples), labeling, packaging, repackaging, compounding, and sales to practitioners
4.2 Recordkeeping in compliance with legal requirements, including content, inventory, maintenance, storage, handling, and reporting: • 4.2.1 Non-dispensing requirements for operations of pharmacies or practice settings • 4.2.2 Possession, storage, and handling of non-hazardous drugs • 4.2.3 Training, possession, handling, storage, and disposal of hazardous drugs • 4.2.4 Allowing non-pharmacist personnel access to drugs • 4.2.5 Requirements for conducting controlled substance inventories	1.7 Procedures for keeping records of information related to pharmacy practice, pharmaceutical products, and patients, including requirements for protecting patient confidentiality • 1.7.1 Requirements pertaining to controlled substance inventories • 1.7.2 Content, maintenance, storage, and reporting requirements for records required in the operation of a pharmacy Prescription filing systems, computer systems and backups, and prescription monitoring programs 2.3.1 Requirements for the operation of a pharmacy or practice setting that is not directly related to the dispensing of pharmaceutical products Issues related to space, equipment, advertising and signage, security (including temporary absence of the pharmacist), policies and procedures, libraries, and references (including veterinary), and the display of licenses 2.3.2 Requirements for the possession, storage, and handling of pharmaceutical products, preparations, bulk drug substances/excipients, and devices, including controlled substances Investigational new drugs, repackaged or resold drugs, sample pharmaceuticals, recalls, and outdated pharmaceutical products *(continued)*

2023 MPJE Competency Statements	Related Previous MPJE Competency Statements
Area 4: Pharmacy Operations (approximately 21% of the exam)	
(*continued*)	1.8 Requirements for handling hazardous materials such as described in USP 800
	• 1.8.1 Requirements for appropriate disposal of hazardous materials
	• 1.8.2 Requirements for training regarding hazardous materials Reverse distributors, quarantine procedures, comprehensive safety programs, and Material Safety Data Sheets
	• 1.8.3 Environmental controls addressing the proper storage, handling, and disposal of hazardous materials Ventilation controls, personal protective equipment, work practices, and reporting
	1.4.12 Procedures and requirements for systems or processes whereby a non-pharmacist may obtain pharmaceutical products, preparations, bulk substances/excipients, and devices Pyxis (vending), after-hour's access, telepharmacies, and secure automated patient drug retrieval centers
	1.4.10 Requirements for emergency kits Supplying, maintenance, access, security, and inventory *Note: This competency statement may be included under allowing non-pharmacist access to drugs*
4.3 Delivery of drugs	2.3.3 Requirements for delivery of pharmaceutical products, preparations, bulk drug substances/excipients, and devices, including controlled substances Issues related to identification of the person accepting delivery of a drug, use of the mail, contract delivery, use of couriers, use of pharmacy employees, use of kiosks, secure mailboxes, script centers, use of vacuum tubes, and use of drive-up windows

2023 MPJE Competency Statements	Related Previous MPJE Competency Statements
Area 4: Pharmacy Operations (approximately 21% of the exam) (*continued*)	
4.4 Conditions for permitted or mandated product selection	1.4.5 Conditions under which product selection is permitted or mandated Consent of the patient and/or prescriber, passing-on of cost savings, and appropriate documentation
4.5 Compounding sterile, nonsterile, hazardous, and non-hazardous preparations	1.4.9 Requirements for compounding pharmaceutical products Environmental controls, release checks and testing, beyond-use date (BUD), and initial and on-going training 1.8.4 Methods for the compounding, dispensing, and administration of hazardous material All hazardous material including sterile and nonsterile compounding
4.6 Centralized prescription processing or central-fill pharmacy dispensing	1.4.13 Procedures and requirements for establishing and operating central processing and central fill pharmacies Remote order verification
4.7 Requirements for the registration, licensure, certification, or permitting of a practice setting or business entity: • 4.7.1 Requirements for registration, license, certification, or permitting of a practice setting • 4.7.2 Requirements for the renewal or reinstatement of a license, registration, certificate, or permit of a practice setting • 4.7.3 Requirements for an inspection of a licensed, registered, certified, or permitted practice setting • 4.7.4 Classifications and processes of disciplinary actions that may be taken against a registered, licensed, certified, or permitted practice setting	2.2 Requirements and application procedure for the registration, licensure, certification, or permitting of a practice setting or business entity • 2.2.1 Requirements for registration, license, certification, or permitting of a practice setting In-state pharmacies, out-of-state pharmacies, specialty pharmacies, controlled substance registrants, wholesalers, distributors, manufacturers/repackagers, computer service providers, and internet pharmacies • 2.2.2 Requirements for an inspection of a licensed, registered, certified, or permitted practice setting • 2.2.3 Requirements for the renewal or reinstatement of a license, registration, certificate, or permit of a practice setting • 2.2.4 Classifications and processes of disciplinary actions that may be taken against a registered, licensed, certified, or permitted practice setting

MPJE® Competency Statements
Effective March 1, 2023

Area 1 | Licensure/Personnel (approximately 22% of the exam)

1.1 **Responsibilities of the pharmacist and non-pharmacist personnel:**

1.1.1 **Qualifications, scope of duties, limitations and restrictions of duties, or conditions to practice for pharmacists-in-charge (or equivalent) and pharmacists**

1.1.2 **Qualifications, scope of duties, limitations, and restrictions of duties, or conditions to practice for non-pharmacist personnel**

These competency statements require you to have a thorough understanding of the legal responsibilities of different personnel. Statement 1.1.1 focuses on the pharmacist-in-charge (or equivalent) and pharmacists. Statement 1.1.2 focuses on non-pharmacist personnel which includes interns, pharmacy owners, and pharmacy technicians all of which were listed in previous competency statements. Most states use the term "pharmacist-in-charge" to indicate the pharmacist who is responsible for the legal operation of a pharmacy, but some states may use other terms. While all pharmacists are responsible for complying with the law, many states will list additional responsibilities for the pharmacist-in-charge. Often, they are responsible for things such as training and establishing policies and procedures. You should make special note of any listed responsibilities for the pharmacist-in-charge that are different from those listed for pharmacists. Another requirement to master these competencies is understanding the responsibilities of pharmacist interns. This requires understanding the specific tasks a pharmacist intern can and cannot do. This will vary by state, but make sure you review whether pharmacist interns can perform activities such as counseling patients, administering immunizations, taking new verbal prescriptions, transferring prescriptions, or performing the final check on a prescription. These are all things you should review under your state law. In addition, you should be familiar with what happens when an intern is working in a pharmacy but is not under the supervision of a preceptor. Does this change the types of activities an intern can or cannot do? Some states address this specific question in their rules, but others may not, so you must deduce the answer based on the wording of the rules. Pharmacy owners may also have specific legal requirements, and those should be studied and contrasted with the other personnel listed.

You need to have a thorough understanding of the duties and activities that pharmacy technicians can and cannot perform under your state law. You should study this section in conjunction with the responsibilities and duties of pharmacists and interns because the duties pharmacists and interns are authorized to perform are often the ones pharmacy technicians cannot perform. It is not enough to just memorize the list of things a pharmacy technician can or cannot do. You must be able to apply that information to specific situations on the MPJE that may not be straightforward. For example, "interpreting a prescription" may be a function only a pharmacist can perform, but what exactly does that mean in practice? Data entry is not generally considered "interpreting a prescription." But other activities may not be as clear. Can a pharmacy technician get clarification from the prescriber on what is written, or is that considered "interpreting a prescription"? Some states make such distinctions clear in their rules, but others require you to determine whether that is something that requires the knowledge and expertise of a pharmacist. Another example would be overriding an alert such as a drug interaction alert. Generally, that is not an activity that a pharmacy technician can perform. It requires a pharmacist to make a determination as to whether an alert like that can be overridden when filling a prescription.

These competency statements also require you to know personnel ratios if they apply in your state. These ratios are most often the ratio of pharmacy technicians to pharmacists that can work in a pharmacy. Many states have eliminated these ratios, but other states still have them, and they can be surprisingly complicated and variable in some states. The ratio is listed as the maximum number of pharmacy technicians who can work under the supervision of a single pharmacist, so they are usually listed as ratios of 2:1, 3:1, 6:1, 8:1, etc. Some states have different ratios depending on the type of pharmacy or the types of activities the pharmacy technicians are involved with. For example, a state may allow a ratio of 6 pharmacy technicians per pharmacist (6:1) but reduce the ratio to 3 pharmacy technicians per pharmacist (3:1) if the pharmacy technicians are engaged in sterile compounding. States may also begin to modify their ratio rules based on the level of pharmacy technician certification.

You should also compare and contrast the activities other non-pharmacy personnel may perform. A cashier, for example, may be allowed to complete a sale, but may not be authorized to perform data entry of prescriptions. Many states also recognize pharmacy technicians in training and may limit the types of activities these individuals may perform until they are licensed or registered as pharmacy technicians.

1.2 Licensures, registrations, and certifications for pharmacists or non-pharmacist personnel:

1.2.1 Qualifications, examinations, internships, maintaining pharmacist competency, and renewals of licensures, registrations, or certifications

These competency statements cover the details required for individuals (as opposed to facilities or locations) to be licensed, registered, or certified. The MPJE is likely to focus on the licensure requirements for pharmacists, but the competency statement requires you to be familiar with the requirements for non-pharmacists such as interns and pharmacy technicians as well. The previous competency statement specifically included preceptors, specialty pharmacist licenses such as nuclear pharmacists, and consultant pharmacists (if those are recognized in your state).

You should focus on the specific items mentioned in the competency statement when reviewing this information under your state laws or rules. This includes qualifications, examinations, and internships. I would not expect questions on licensing fees as fees are always changing, but you should know the requirements for licensure, including things such as hours of internship required, certification and additional educational requirements for preceptors, and specialty licenses such as those for nuclear pharmacists.

The inclusion of "maintaining pharmacist competency" deals with rules related to maintaining professional competency. This is primarily done through mandating continuing education. The rules for continuing education vary in each state, but you need to be familiar with the details regarding these requirements. In addition to knowing the number of continuing education hours a pharmacist must complete to renew their license, you should be familiar with methods of obtaining continuing education; requirements for specific topics such as law, medication errors, or controlled substances; and any requirements for live courses or seminars. Often, to perform certain activities, specific continuing education requirements must be met. Pharmacists who serve as preceptors may need continuing education related to preceptor training. Similarly, mandatory continuing education may be required for sterile compounding, immunizations and vaccinations, collaborative practice, medication therapy management, laboratory testing, etc. You should also know the requirements for continuing education for new pharmacists upon their initial renewal. All states recognize continuing education courses that are accredited by the Accreditation Council for Pharmacy Education (ACPE). ACPE uses continuing education units (CEUs) instead of continuing education hours when accrediting courses. A 3-hour continuing education course would be listed by ACPE as 0.3 CEUs. Continuing education provided by ACPE-approved providers is tracked by NABP through NABP's CPE Monitor. All pharmacists should obtain an NABP CPE Monitor number and provide that number when registering for an ACPE-approved continuing education course.

1.2.2 Classifications and processes of disciplinary actions

The classifications of disciplinary actions that may be taken against licensees will vary by state. Although the terminology may vary by state, disciplinary actions usually include reprimands, suspensions, and revocations, with revocation being the most serious. Boards can also place restrictions on licensees and assess fines or administrative penalties as part of the disciplinary process. Fines and penalties may be assessed in conjunction with the other sanctions against the licensee. Some states can also take action that is considered non-disciplinary such as the issuing of citations or letters of deficiencies. The process for a board of pharmacy to take disciplinary action will also vary by state. These rules are often quite technical, with lots of legal language, and can be difficult to understand. Some boards provide summaries of the disciplinary process on their websites and reviewing that type of information can make these requirements easier to understand.

1.2.3 Reporting to and participating in programs addressing the inability to practice with reasonable skill and safety

This competency statement deals with programs related to inability to practice safely due to an impairment, primarily drug and alcohol impairment. It includes any mandatory requirements a state may have to report a pharmacist, pharmacy technician, or other health-care provider who may be unable to practice safely due to an impairment. Requirements can be mandatory reporting to a board or may include mandatory referral to a professional recovery program. You should be familiar with the reporting requirements in this area as well as the details of participation in any pharmacist recovery program or professional recovery program in your state.

Area 2 | Pharmacist Practice (approximately 33% of the exam)

2.1   Requirements for issuing prescriptions/drug orders:

The key word in all the competencies under 2.1 may be the word "issuing." These competency statements are about the legality of the prescription when it is "issued." This means knowing which practitioners can prescribe, which drug categories they can prescribe, and any limitations on their prescribing based either on their type of license or specific limitations for certain drug classes. More detail is provided below.

2.1.1   Requirements for drug uses, limitations, or restrictions

This competency statement includes any specific requirements for issuing a prescription/drug order that may exist for specific products. This could also include requirements under a Risk Evaluation and Mitigation Strategy (REMS). *See discussion of REMS in Chapter 2.*

Other requirements, limitations, or restrictions include methadone programs and office-based opioid treatment programs. It is important to understand that methadone prescriptions cannot be filled in a pharmacy unless the methadone is being prescribed for pain. *See discussion of methadone and narcotic treatment centers in Chapter 3.* Office-based opioid treatment programs have limitations on the prescribing and dispensing of buprenorphine and buprenorphine/naloxone by DATA-waived practitioners to treat opioid addiction. This is also referred to as Medication Assisted Therapy (MAT). *See details in Chapter 3.*

More broadly, an obvious limitation under this competency is that all prescriptions must be issued for a legitimate medical purpose and in the usual course of professional practice. There is a specific federal rule for this for controlled substances, but this is true for non-controlled substances as well. States may have specific rules to make this clear, but even if they do not, you would not want to fill a prescription that was not written for a legitimate medical purpose or one that was not issued in the usual course of professional practice. Other limitations may be related to scope of practice, but this is more specifically addressed in competency statement 2.1.2 below.

Finally, this competency likely includes any quantity limitations for specific therapeutic categories. Various states have implemented limitations on prescriptions for certain types of drugs. This is most frequently seen with controlled substances for drugs, such as opioids for acute pain, benzodiazepines, or even drugs to treat weight loss. You should be familiar with any such limitations in your state. As discussed in one of the Study Tips in Chapter 3, it is important that you are certain that any quantity limitations are required by law. Restrictions based on a specific company's policy or from insurance companies are not legal requirements and could cause you to choose the incorrect answer on the MPJE.

2.1.2 Scope of authority, scope of practice, limitations or restrictions of practice, and valid registration of practitioners who are authorized to prescribe, dispense, or administer drugs

This competency statement is focused on who can legally issue prescriptions and which prescriptions a pharmacist can fill.

Scope of authority

The scope of authority for a practitioner may be limited by law. For instance, the prescriptive authority of mid-level practitioners such as Advance Practice Registered Nurses (APRNs) and Physician Assistants (PAs) may be limited. Some states may allow these types of practitioners to prescribe only non-controlled substances, some states may allow them to prescribe some controlled substances, and some states may allow them to prescribe all controlled substances. Similarly, some states may authorize certain types of practitioners prescriptive authority, such as optometrists or even pharmacists, but the scope of that authority may be limited to a specific formulary or have other restrictions. State laws may also impose days' supply limits for certain types of practitioners. You must know the specific limitations and scope of authority for each type of practitioner in your state.

Scope of practice

Limitations based on scope of practice have to do with the type of license the practitioner has. For example, dentists may only prescribe drugs if they are treating the patient for a dental issue, and podiatrists may only prescribe drugs to treat problems associated with the feet. Likewise, veterinarians may not prescribe for humans and medical doctors may not prescribe for animals. Be careful not to confuse scope of practice issues with specialty areas of practice. Physicians, both medical doctors (M.D.s) and osteopathic physicians (D.O.s), can treat people. They may have chosen to specialize in a certain area of medicine, but that does not mean it is illegal for them to prescribe outside of their specialty area. Thus, while a prescription from a dentist for birth control pills would not be valid because it is outside the scope of practice for a dentist, a prescription for birth control pills written by an M.D. who is a cardiologist would not necessarily be considered illegal. It would be unusual because it is outside of the physician's specialty area, but it would not be per se illegal. The best practice would be to seek more information before filling such a prescription to ensure that it was written for a legitimate medical purpose and in the usual course of professional practice.

Valid registration

Obviously, for a prescription to be valid, the prescriber must have a valid license and, if the prescription is for a controlled substance, a valid DEA registration. A valid state-controlled substance registration may be needed in some jurisdictions. Be aware that a DEA registration could limit a practitioner's ability to prescribe, possess, or administer certain schedules of controlled substances. *See discussion on DEA registrations in Chapter 3.*

Other topics that may be included in this competency include limitations on jurisdictional prescribing and internet prescribing.

Limits on jurisdictional prescribing

This requires you to know if prescriptions issued by practitioners from other states and even other countries are valid and can be filled in your state. This can be complicated because it may depend on the type of practitioner, the type of drug being prescribed (e.g., controlled substance or non-controlled substance), how the prescription is issued (e.g., written, verbal, electronic), and where the practitioner is located. It may be helpful to create a chart outlining the many different scenarios that could apply or check to see if the board of pharmacy in your state already has such a chart. As for prescriptions from outside the country, unless your state specifically recognizes practitioners in other countries, it is unlikely that such prescriptions would be considered legal.

Internet prescribing

This one is a bit tricky because DEA and many states adopted rules that prohibited prescriptions that were issued based on internet questionnaires without at least one valid in-person physical examination. *See discussion on Ryan Haight Act in Chapter 3.* However, more recently, telemedicine has become widespread, and prescriptions issued by practitioners based on a telemedicine visit (which is likely accomplished through the internet) may be valid. Some states have placed limitations on certain types of prescriptions that were issued based on telemedicine, so you should be familiar with any such restrictions.

2.1.3   Requirements for issuing non-controlled prescriptions/drug orders

2.1.4   Requirements for issuing controlled prescriptions/drug orders

These two competency statements require you to know the detailed required elements for prescriptions and medication orders. Even though many states are moving toward mandatory electronic prescriptions for either controlled substances or for all prescriptions, there are always exceptions to those mandates, so it is important to know the required elements on prescriptions and medication orders for each type of transmission: written, telephonic, facsimile, and electronic.

DEA rules dictate the minimum requirements for prescriptions for controlled substances, and this information is covered in Chapter 3. Be sure to check for any additional requirements under your state law for controlled substance prescriptions. You should also make note of any requirements that are different for alternative modes of transmission. For instance, a faxed prescription may require the name or identification of the person who transmitted the prescription.

Other topics that were in previous competency statements that may be included under this competency include: requirements for issuing a prescription during an emergency, tamper-evident prescription forms, time limits for filling initial prescription/drug orders, and issuing multiple Schedule II prescriptions.

Tamper-evident prescription forms

Tamper-evident prescription forms are required for Medicaid prescriptions as discussed in Chapter 2, but many states also require tamper-evident prescription forms for written prescriptions for either all controlled substances or for Schedule II controlled substances.

Time limits for filling initial prescriptions/drug orders

This would include time limits for filling initial prescriptions for controlled substances as discussed in Chapter 3, but some states may have a limitation on non-controlled substances as well. If a state law specifies that prescriptions may not be refilled for more than one year, that implies that the initial dispensing must also occur within one year.

Requirements for issuing multiple Schedule II prescriptions

This is a topic that causes much confusion. *See the detailed discussion on this in Chapter 3.*

2.1.5 Authority limitations of practitioners' ability to authorize refills

This competency includes limitations that apply to all practitioners such as limitations on refills permitted on Schedule III–V controlled substances. It also includes any limitations placed on different types of practitioners under state law. Previous versions of this competency statement specifically included how to handle refills of prescriptions from a retired or deceased practitioner. It is difficult to tell if this is still a topic that could still be included on the exam, but given the broad language in the new competency statements it is a possibility. Not every state will address this in their rules or regulations. Some states may address it through informal policy statements, so you may have to do some research on this issue in your state. From a strict legal view, it would seem logical that if a prescriber is no longer actively practicing or is deceased, his or her prescriptions are no longer valid. DEA Rule 1301.52(a) states that a DEA registration terminates when a practitioner dies. It makes sense that any refills remaining on a prescription are no longer valid once a practitioner is deceased or retired. This may be the best legal answer, but it does not really take care of the patient. Several states have adopted rules or policies to address these situations. If your state has not adopted a rule or policy on this, it is difficult to advise you on how to address a question on this for your state. In practice, I recommend using the emergency refill rules if your state has them and the facts of the situation support the use of those rules. Providing an emergency refill allows the patient to continue their therapy and hopefully prevent patient harm. However, since the MPJE is testing you on the law, unless your state specifically addresses this issue in rules or guidance documents, it is recommended you answer a question on this based on the strict legal view that says any prescription or refills are no longer valid after the prescriber is retired or deceased.

2.2 Conditions under which the pharmacist or non-pharmacist personnel participates in the administration of drugs in the management of patients' therapy

This competency statement is nearly identical to previous competency 1.3.3, but the previous competency included the word "or" after the words "administration of drugs." This means it previously included a broader range of activities related to management of patient's drug therapy. It is unclear if this is a typo in the 2023 MPJE Competencies or if they intentionally wanted to limit this competency to only rules regarding the administration of drugs. The previous competency specifically included other non-dispensing activities such as prescriptive authority, collaborative practice, consulting, counseling (now included in 2.3), medication administration (including immunizations and vaccines), ordering labs, medication therapy management, and disease state management. It is not likely that these topics would be excluded from the MPJE, so I am including a discussion of some of these topics. Other topics are covered elsewhere.

Administering drugs including immunizations and vaccinations

The authority for pharmacists to administer drugs (including immunizations and vaccinations) varies greatly among the states, including which drugs and immunizations or vaccines can be administered, age limitations, requirements for training, certification, continuing education, protocols, notifications, and documentation. You need to know all these details under state law. Some states have extended the ability to administer immunizations and vaccines to interns and pharmacy technicians as well. Differences in the authorities between pharmacists and other personnel should be noted. States may also have other specific requirements for individuals providing immunizations or administering drugs, such as professional liability insurance or certification.

In response to the COVID-19 pandemic, authorizations under the federal Public Readiness and Emergency Preparedness (PREP) Act allow all pharmacists to independently order and administer COVID-19 vaccines, and all Centers for Disease Control and Prevention (CDC) Advisory Committee on Immunization Practices (ACIP) recommended childhood vaccines, regardless of state law. Additional authorizations under the PREP Act permit pharmacy technicians with appropriate training to administer COVID-19 vaccinations irrespective of state laws and regulations. This authority was extended for flu vaccines provided to adults 19 years of age or older in 2021. Other PREP Act authorities include the ordering and administering of COVID-19 point-of-care tests and expanding the scope of authority for licensed pharmacists to order and administer, and for qualified pharmacy technicians and pharmacy interns to administer COVID-19 therapeutics subcutaneously, intramuscularly, or orally. These authorities under the federal PREP Act are temporary, and if not extended are scheduled to expire in October 2024. It is not likely the MPJE would ask questions based on temporary authorities under the PREP Act, but you should check to see if your state has made some of the provisions of the PREP Act permanent under state law.

You should also be familiar with pharmacists or other individuals' authority to administer epinephrine auto-injectors, which sometimes is part of the same rules for immunizations and vaccinations, so that a pharmacist can administer epinephrine in case a patient has an allergic reaction to a vaccination.

Prescriptive authority

Only a few states give pharmacists independent prescriptive authority—that is, allowing a pharmacist to prescribe drugs without some type of collaborative practice agreement or protocol with a physician. The most common exception is a limited ability to prescribe and dispense naloxone, but even that usually requires some type of standing order from a physician. In the few states that do allow some type of pharmacist prescribing, you should know the details of what types of drugs can be prescribed, any limitations, any required training or certification, and the proper procedures and recordkeeping requirements. According to the 2022 NABP Survey of Pharmacy Law, 15 states recognize some type of independent prescribing by pharmacists outside of collaborative practice or under a protocol. Most of these authorities are limited to specific drugs or devices, with the most common being naloxone or oral contraceptives.

The Emergency Use Authorization for Paxlovid®, issued by FDA on July 6, 2022, authorizes all state-licensed pharmacists to prescribe Paxlovid® (with certain limitations) to expand access to timely treatment for some patients who are eligible to receive this drug for the treatment of COVID-19. There are several practical problems with this authorization as it requires pharmacists (but not other prescribers) to have information available about the patient's hepatic and renal function that is not more than 12 months old, and a comprehensive list of medications (both prescribed and nonprescribed) that the patient is taking.

Note: This is the first time that FDA has ever authorized a drug with different requirements for distinct types of prescribers. That may be because this is only under an Emergency Use Authorization for Paxlovid® and not the final approval for the drug.

Collaborative practice

Many states have laws that allow some type of collaborative practice between a pharmacist and a physician, often through a collaborative practice agreement. These agreements authorize the pharmacist to perform certain patient care activities on behalf of the practitioner, which may include some type of prescriptive authority in some states. The practitioner is most commonly a physician, but some states may authorize collaborative practice agreements between a pharmacist and other types of prescribers. States may use different terminology to describe these agreements, including collaborative care agreements, collaborative drug therapy management agreements, drug therapy management agreements under protocol, consult agreements, etc. Some states have different rules for drug therapy management and collaborative practice, so be sure to review both practices, which are similar but could have minor differences. Collaborative practice agreements often authorize the pharmacist to implement, modify, or discontinue drug therapy, and order and interpret laboratory tests. While nearly every state has some type of collaborative practice law, the extent of the pharmacist's authority and the requirements and limitations vary greatly.

You should be familiar with the details of any collaborative practice laws or medication therapy management laws in your state, including qualifications, requirements for continuing education, protocols, supervision, documentation, and recordkeeping. You should also take note of any limitations to certain practice settings and the scope of authorized activities.

2.3   Requirements regarding counseling:

2.3.1   Counseling or offering to counsel

2.3.2   Documenting counseling or documenting offering to counsel

The original federal rules under OBRA 90 required pharmacists to make an offer to counsel and perform drug utilization reviews for Medicaid patients. *Note: There was no Medicare drug coverage at that time.* Every state has adopted these requirements in different ways, with some making them applicable to all patients and some making them applicable only to Medicaid patients. Some states also made patient counseling mandatory, while others maintained the OBRA 90 requirement of providing an offer to counsel. You need to have a good understanding of the counseling requirements in your state. Is it an offer to counsel or is it mandatory counseling? Is it required for new prescriptions only or also for refills? Are the elements of the counseling mandated, or is it up to the pharmacist to determine what to counsel about? What documentation is required? What happens when a patient refuses counseling? How is counseling accomplished if the prescription is delivered?

The original federal rules under OBRA 90 also required pharmacists to document their comments in performing these activities. The rules state these comments would be considered reasonable if an impartial observer could review the documentation and understand what has occurred in the past, including what the pharmacist told the patient, information discovered about the patient, and what the pharmacist thought of the patient's drug therapy. Many states have specific rules regarding documentation of counseling, offers to counsel, refusals to accept counseling, or for drug utilization review, but even in the absence of specific state rules, this original federal rule could be considered a requirement for documentation of patient counseling.

2.4   Returning or reusing drugs

Generally, pharmaceutical products that have been dispensed cannot be returned and reused, but there are often different rules for drugs that have been dispensed to patients in nursing homes or similar facilities. Some states may allow the return of non-controlled substances from these facilities to be reused if certain conditions are met. Be sure to review any such rules in your state and the specific conditions that must be met for this to occur.

Other issues that were specifically included under this competency in the past include charitable programs, cancer or other repository programs, previously dispensed, and from "will call" areas of pharmacies. These are addressed below.

"Will call" areas of pharmacy

Drugs that are not picked up by patients and remain in the "will call" area of the pharmacy have not left the pharmacy department and are usually not considered to have been dispensed. Therefore, many states allow these drugs to be reused. They should not be mixed in with other stock bottles on the shelf, however, as this would cause mixing of lot numbers, making the stock bottle misbranded. Be sure to check any specific requirements in your state regarding return to stock of drugs in the will call bin.

Charitable programs, cancer, or other repository programs

Approximately 13 states have cancer drug repository programs. These programs are intended to address prescription drug waste by allowing unused cancer drugs that have been dispensed in a closed system (such as in a nursing home) to be reused. They usually exclude controlled substances, expired drugs, and drugs that may be adulterated or misbranded. They often require a pharmacist to inspect the drugs prior to being reused and provide liability protections to the donors and recipients of the drugs. Some states also have similar charitable drug programs that expand beyond cancer drugs.

2.5 Regulations and agencies regarding pharmacy practice:

2.5.1 Requirements for promoting quality and safety of public health

This is such a broad statement it literally could encompass any FDA or Board of Pharmacy rule, as these agencies are charged with promoting the quality and safety of public health. I have included a discussion of several topics that were previously specifically mentioned in the competency statements that could fit under this broader statement.

Risk Evaluation and Mitigation Strategies (REMS)

REMS arguably could be included under this competency statement as they are requirements that apply to certain drugs or drug categories to promote the safe use of those products. *A detailed discussion of REMS can be found in Chapter 2.*

Patient Package Inserts and FDA Medication Guides

FDA requirements for Patient Package Inserts and Medication Guides may be included under this competency statement. *See Chapter 2 for a discussion of both.*

Written drug information

States may have specific requirements for written drug information separate from the federal requirements of Patient Package Inserts and FDA Medication Guides. These are often part of the requirements for patient counseling, which may require written information to be provided with prescriptions in addition to verbal counseling or an offer to counsel. Even in states that do not have mandatory patient counseling and only require an offer to counsel, the requirement to provide written information may be mandatory.

Quality assurance programs (including peer review)

These programs are sometimes called "Continuous Quality Improvement" (CQI) programs. Quality assurance programs, peer review programs, and CQI programs are all programs that some states either mandate or encourage pharmacies to implement. The intent is to require or encourage pharmacies to have quality committees or peer review committees to review errors (or near errors) that occur in a pharmacy to try to prevent such errors from occurring in the future. States may use different terminology when describing the types of events that would be reviewed (such as quality-related events or medication-related events), but they would always include any medication or dispensing errors. These programs try to determine the root cause of an error and make the appropriate changes in the pharmacy to minimize the chance of the error occurring again.

One of the keys to any quality improvement program or peer review program is making sure that the information from the investigation and analysis of the errors remains confidential and is not subject to discovery in any lawsuit. When these laws are passed, they have legal protections to prevent the findings of the committee from being released in a lawsuit. Without such protection, pharmacies would be hesitant to implement one of these programs and create that type of documentation.

Some states mandate that all pharmacies have a CQI program. Other states have authorized pharmacies to have such programs, but they are not mandated. However, even if they are not mandated for every pharmacy, some boards of pharmacy will mandate that a pharmacy implement such a program after a medication error has occurred.

Error reporting

Mandatory error reporting is less common than you might think. Most error reporting systems are voluntary. FDA's program for medication error reporting, MedWatch, receives over 100,000 reports of suspected medication errors per year, but most of those reports are made voluntarily. Only drug manufacturers and a few others have mandated reporting requirements to MedWatch. Reports from healthcare practitioners, including pharmacists, to MedWatch are voluntary.

Another voluntary medication error reporting program is the Institute for Safe Medication Practices Medication Error Reporting Program (ISMP-MERP). There is also a National Coordinating Council for Medication Error Reporting and Prevention (NCC-MERP). This council is a group of over 20 organizations that work together to maximize the safe use of medications and to increase awareness of medication errors through open communication, increased reporting, and promotion of medication error prevention strategies. These are great programs, but because they are voluntary, they are not likely to be on the MPJE.

Mandatory error reporting requirements are usually enacted by states and most commonly require reporting of errors causing serious injury or death. These requirements usually only apply in hospital practice, and they may not be just for errors related to medication errors. There are a few states that specifically require reporting of serious medication errors to the state board of pharmacy.

Public health reporting requirements

Many states have requirements for mandatory reporting by pharmacies related to public health. These may include a potential terrorist event, physical abuse, and treatment for tuberculosis. These mandatory reports are generally made to public health authorities and not the state board of pharmacy. The rules related to a potential terrorist event are likely to be related to bioterrorism, where a pharmacy is observing an increase in prescriptions for antibiotics or drugs to treat respiratory or gastrointestinal complaints. There may be similar reporting requirements to help identify tuberculosis or other highly contagious diseases with the goal of early detection of an epidemic or pandemic. As healthcare professionals, pharmacists may also have mandatory reporting requirements related to suspected physical abuse.

Drug paraphernalia

Drug paraphernalia laws primarily impact a pharmacy as they relate to sales of needles and syringes. You should determine whether your state requires a prescription to dispense needles and syringes and, if they do, whether there are any exceptions. In the past, drug paraphernalia laws restricted the sales of needles and syringes, but states began to eliminate or modify those laws during the AIDS pandemic to allow easier access to clean syringes. According to the NABP Survey of Pharmacy Law, only four states still require a prescription for needles and syringes, and even in those states there are exceptions. More states limit the quantity that can be purchased without a prescription or require the purchaser to be a certain age. You should take note of any of those requirements in your state laws. Also, a few states restrict the sales of needles and syringes to pharmacies.

Pharmacists' responsibilities in Medicare-certified skilled nursing facilities

This is primarily related to a Medicare requirement that a consultant pharmacist perform a Medication Regimen Review for long-term care patients every 30 days. *See Chapter 3.*

2.5.2   Protecting patient and health record confidentiality

You should be familiar with any pharmacy-specific rules in your state related to confidentiality. In addition, you should have a general understanding of how the privacy and security rules under the Health Insurance Portability and Accountability Act (HIPAA) impact the use and disclosure of protected health information in a pharmacy. *A summary of HIPAA can be found in Chapter 2.*

Area 3 | Dispensing Requirements
(approximately 24% of the exam)

3.1 **Responsibilities for determining whether prescriptions/drug orders are issued for a legitimate medical purpose and within all applicable restrictions**

This competency statement primarily concerns a pharmacist's corresponding responsibility relating to controlled substance prescriptions. *See Chapter 3.*

To be valid, all prescriptions (not just controlled substance prescriptions), must be issued for a legitimate medical purpose and must be based on a valid patient/prescriber relationship. You must be able to determine what constitutes a valid prescriber/patient relationship. This sometimes includes rules related to self-prescribing and prescribing for friends or family members. Some states may have specific rules that prohibit practitioners from self-prescribing or for prescribing for family members, particularly for controlled substances. Surprisingly, the Federal Controlled Substances Act (FCSA) does not directly address the issue. The FCSA only states that, to be legal, a prescription must be issued based on a valid practitioner/patient relationship and in the usual course of professional practice. One of the primary indicators that there is a valid practitioner/patient relationship is that the practitioner retains records regarding the patient. This would prohibit a practitioner from prescribing for a friend or family member unless the practitioner maintains records for the friend or family member. This is a difficult area because the pharmacist may not know the details under which the prescription was issued, but pharmacists must use their professional judgment. For the MPJE, you should research if there are any specific laws, rules, policy statements, or guidance documents that address these situations in your state.

This competency statement may include other topics that fall under "restrictions," although "restrictions" are also mentioned in statement 2.1.1. One such restriction may be maximum quantities that can be dispensed for certain types of prescriptions. This is most frequently seen with certain controlled substance prescriptions. *See Chapter 3.* Quantity limitations may also apply under certain REMS programs. Be sure you answer any questions on maximum quantities based on the actual laws and rules and not based on limitations from insurance companies, pharmacy benefit managers, or store policies.

3.2 Transferring prescription/drug order information between pharmacies by authorized personnel

The rules regarding the transfer of prescriptions are a surprisingly misunderstood area of pharmacy law. Part of the reason for this is there has been confusion within the profession as to how DEA interprets their own rules regarding transfers of controlled substances, particularly the transfer of original controlled substance prescriptions. *See discussion in Chapter 3.*

You should also review your state laws and rules on the required procedures to transfer a prescription from one pharmacy to another. These rules were written many years ago, when most prescriptions were issued in writing rather than electronically. Even though many prescriptions are issued electronically today and transfers can also be done electronically, you should be familiar with the process of transferring prescriptions manually. This includes any specific documentation required to be made on the physical copy of the prescription. Some states also make it a violation for a pharmacist or pharmacy to refuse to transfer a prescription or may require that transfers be completed within a certain time period. Be sure to review whether pharmacy technicians or interns can be involved in transferring prescriptions.

3.3 Prospective drug utilization reviews:

Drug utilization review was required for Medicaid patients as part of OBRA 90, as discussed under patient counseling above. Most states require pharmacists to perform a drug utilization review for all prescriptions, not just Medicaid prescriptions. As part of the drug utilization review, OBRA 90 requires screening for:

- Therapeutic duplication
- Drug-disease contraindication
- Drug-drug interactions
- Incorrect drug dosage
- Incorrect duration of treatment
- Drug-allergy interactions
- Clinical abuse/misuse of medication

Some states call this "drug regimen review," and the terms are sometimes used interchangeably. Drug regimen review is often used to denote a prospective review as it is intended to be done prior to the dispensing of a new prescription. Drug utilization review is sometimes considered to be retrospective rather than prospective. You should review your state requirements relating to drug utilization review and/or drug regimen review.

3.3.1 Requirements for reporting to PMP and accessing PMP data

This is another form of drug utilization review because the purpose of prescription monitoring programs is to allow pharmacists and prescribers to review a complete profile of controlled substances that have been prescribed or dispensed to a patient.

You should be familiar with the required elements reported to the state prescription monitoring program, the confidentiality of the PMP information, and what is considered legitimate access. *See general discussion of PMP programs in Chapter 3.*

3.4 Exceptions to dispensing or refilling prescriptions/drug orders

This is one of the most difficult competency statements to understand. It is unclear to me what is meant by the term "exceptions." My best guess is this is similar to the previous competency statement 1.4.3 that included conditions under which a prescription/order may be filled or refilled. That competency statement specifically listed emergency fills or refills, partial dispensing of a controlled substance, disaster or emergency protocol, patient identification, requirement for death with dignity, medical marijuana, and conscience/moral circumstances. These are discussed below.

Emergency fills or refills

Many states have rules that allow a pharmacist to dispense an emergency refill in circumstances where the pharmacist is unable to get authorization for a refill from the prescriber, and failure to provide the medication may result in interruption of a patient's therapy. These rules require the pharmacist to use their professional judgment, but you should be familiar with the requirements and limitations that apply based on your state law. Most often, these state laws allow a specific days' supply of an emergency refill, such as a 72-hour supply. You should also determine if there are any restrictions for specific types of drugs such as controlled substances or specific therapeutic classes. There are situations where you may not be able to comply with the law exactly. For instance, if the law only authorizes a 72-hour supply for an emergency refill, how do you provide an emergency refill of a prescription for eye drops or an inhaler? Some states specifically address these situations and authorize dispensing these unit-of-use products even though they may be more than the days' supply allowed, but other states may not address these situations.

Partial dispensing of a controlled substance

See Chapter 3.

Disaster or emergency protocol

This is related to the emergency refill rules, as many states often extend the days' supply limit for emergency refills during emergencies or disasters. They often require that there be an emergency declaration or disaster declaration issued by the state or the governor's office and will usually specify the conditions that will allow a pharmacist to provide emergency refills for an extended time (often 30 days). During disasters or other emergencies, states may also waive certain rules or allow pharmacists to dispense drugs at temporary locations.

Patient identification

There is no requirement to obtain patient identification when dispensing a controlled substance under the FCSA, but many states have identification requirements, particularly for controlled substance prescriptions. Often there are exceptions, so be sure to note when identification is not required.

Requirements for death with dignity

Death with dignity laws allow certain patients to request a prescription for a medication that will end their life should they choose to take it. Oregon was the first state to pass a death with dignity law, and a total of 8 states and Washington, D.C., now have some form of a death with dignity law. The laws are very stringent, and, in states where this is permitted, you should review the criteria for patients to participate (age, documentation of terminal illness, etc.), the procedures, and the dispensing and documentation requirements.

Medical marijuana

Medical marijuana is no longer specifically mentioned in the MPJE competencies but was included in previous versions. As discussed in the introductory material, when state and federal laws are different, you must follow the stricter law, and if the two laws conflict, the federal law must be followed. Marijuana is still an illegal Schedule I controlled substance under federal law, so all state medical marijuana laws are technically not valid. A pharmacy that dispenses medical marijuana risks losing their DEA registration even if it is legal in a state. There are a few states that have legalized medical marijuana and require a pharmacist to be involved in the dispensing, or where the Board of Pharmacy licenses the medical marijuana dispensaries. If this applies in your state, you should review those rules, but for the majority of states, the dispensing of medical marijuana is not part of the practice of pharmacy, so it is unlikely that this would be a topic on the MPJE in those states.

Conscience/moral circumstances

Conscience clauses are laws that allow healthcare providers to refuse to provide or take part in procedures that violate their religious or personal beliefs or values. They generally come up in the context of abortions, but most often apply to pharmacists in the context of contraception and, more specifically, emergency contraception. Not all states have rules on this, but when they do, they can sometimes take opposite approaches. Some states explicitly grant pharmacists the right to refuse to dispense drugs related to contraception on moral grounds. Other states require pharmacies to fill any legal prescription for birth control or any other medication. In some states, the pharmacist has a right to refuse to fill a prescription, but the law also provides protections for patients by requiring referral to another pharmacy or pharmacist that can ensure patient access. Other states do not provide specific patient protections. You should check to see if your state laws or rules address these issues.

3.5   Labeling of dispensed drugs

Requirements for the labeling of prescriptions are controlled by state law, and they are often quite detailed. In practice, the pharmacy computer system prints out the prescription, but for the MPJE it is important that you know these detailed labeling requirements. Be sure to know all the mandatory elements on a prescription label and any differences for labels for certain practice settings such as nursing homes or hospitals.

If your state has specific rules mandating the use of auxiliary labels, you should review those. Some states have rules mandating additional labeling requirements on some or all prescriptions for things such as how to properly dispose of medication, how to find a drug disposal location, or specific requirements for instructions in other languages. Often, these labeling requirements have specific language that must be used and may be so detailed that the required language will not fit on the prescription drug label. To address this, the rules may allow the information to be provided in an alternative manner, such as a document provided with the prescription or by directing patients to a website to get more information.

3.6   Packaging of dispensed drugs

This competency statement is fairly vague, and it is difficult to understand what they are referring to. It is possible it is focusing on any prescription products that have specialized packaging or components that must be dispensed with the drug product, such as special needles or accessories. The statement could also be referring to products that have special labeling requirements or are required to be dispensed in the manufacturer's original packaging. Some states also have specific requirements on how certain products are dispensed and may not allow certain types of bottles (e.g., glass bottles) or prescription vials for specific drugs. It may also include rules related to child-resistant packaging and customized patient medication packaging. *See Chapter 2 for discussion of both of these topics.*

3.7   Drug product conditions prohibiting dispensing

This competency statement includes a thorough understanding of adulteration and misbranding, although those specific terms were removed from the statement. Adulteration and misbranding are violations of the Food, Drug, and Cosmetic Act, and are often misunderstood. *See Chapter 2 for details.*

Any rules related to "beyond-use" dating for prescription drugs likely fall under this competency as well. You should know your state's rules for beyond-use dating for general prescriptions, customized medication packages, and nonsterile and sterile compounded preparations.

3.8   Requirements for the distribution and/or dispensing of non-prescription pharmaceutical products, including controlled substances and hazardous drugs:

3.8.1   Dispensing or administration

3.8.2   Labeling of nonprescription drugs and devices

3.8.3   Packaging and repackaging of nonprescription drugs and behind-the-counter products

3.8.4 Dispensing restricted, nonprescription drugs

This group of competencies deals with nonprescription products, or over-the-counter (OTC) products, and hazardous drugs. The reference to hazardous drugs in the competency statement may be related to special requirements for these products under the Federal Hazardous Substances Act for products that are considered poisons. Notably, drugs regulated by FDA are excluded under the Federal Hazardous Substances Act. However, if a pharmacy has chemicals or bulk substances that meet the definition of a poison, these rules could apply. *See details in Chapter 2.* Each of the competency statements in this section is discussed below.

Dispensing or administration

By definition, OTC products do not need a prescription to be dispensed or administered, but you should be familiar with how to treat a prescription that is issued for an OTC drug. *This is discussed in Chapter 2.* The competency statement also includes rules related to the selling of Schedule V–exempt narcotics without a prescription. Federal law permits this, although you must check your state law to see if it is allowed. Even in states where this is allowed, it is not done very often in practice, so many pharmacy students and pharmacists are unaware of the specific requirements. *See Chapter 3 for details.*

Labeling of nonprescription drugs and devices

See Chapter 2, including special labeling requirements for certain OTC products.

Packaging and repackaging of nonprescription drugs and behind-the-counter products

See Chapter 2 on the packaging and repackaging of nonprescription drugs.

Dispensing restricted, nonprescription drugs

The most common restricted, nonprescription products include pseudoephedrine, dextromethorphan, and to a lesser degree, emergency contraceptives. Each is discussed below.

Pseudoephedrine

Pseudoephedrine products must be kept behind the counter and have sales limits and other restrictions. *See Chapter 3.*

Dextromethorphan

Some states require products with dextromethorphan to be kept behind the counter or have age restrictions to purchase such products. There is not a federal law on this, so you will need to check the law in your state to see if any such restrictions apply.

Emergency contraception

When single pill levonorgestrel (Plan B One-Step) was first made available without a prescription, it had age restrictions. It was initially only available without a prescription for women aged 17 and older. There was also confusion, political controversy, and lawsuits surrounding the age limitations for Plan B One-Step that are beyond the scope of this book. However, since 2013, Plan B One-Step, and similar generic versions of single dose levonorgestrel, are available without a prescription to anyone, of any age. These products are often kept behind the counter. Next Choice, the two-pill emergency contraceptive option, does have an age restriction. It is available behind the counter without a prescription for women 17 and older. Women under 17 still need a prescription. No states currently restrict the sale of Plan B, but given the overturning of *Roe v. Wade* in *Dobbs v. Jackson Women's Health Organization*, new legislation may be introduced to do so in some states, and there may be legislation to strengthen or expand access in other states.

Area 4 | Pharmacy Operations (Approximately 21% of the Exam)

4.1   Ordering, acquisition, and distribution of drugs, including maintenance and content of such records:

4.1.1   Ordering and acquisition, including the maintenance and content of such records

4.1.2   Distribution, including the maintenance and content of such records

These competency statements are concerned with the "distribution" of prescription drugs, not the "dispensing" of prescription drugs. This is a critical distinction. It illustrates the importance of reading these competency statements carefully and reading MPJE questions carefully. Distribution and dispensing are two separate concepts. Dispensing is nearly always done on a patient-specific basis and the drugs may be dispensed in smaller quantities than the manufacturer's packaging. The ordering and acquisition of drugs is a distribution activity that involves the movement of prescription drugs in the original manufacturer's packaging. This includes pharmacies purchasing drugs from wholesalers or manufacturers, but also includes pharmacies distributing such drugs to other pharmacies, physicians, wholesalers (for returns), and reverse distributors.

The acquisition of pharmaceutical drugs includes how a pharmacy would order drugs. The details regarding the ordering of controlled substances can be found in Chapter 3. In addition, this competency statement includes requirements under the drug track-and-trace requirements of the Drug Supply Chain Security Act (DSCSA). The DSCSA preempted all state laws related to the tracking of drugs, including things like drug pedigrees. This means that even if a state still has laws regarding drug pedigrees or the tracking of pharmaceuticals, those laws are no longer in effect. Only the federal law is in effect to allow a single, uniform system for tracking pharmaceutical products throughout the supply chain. You should be familiar with the details of the DSCSA found in Chapter 2.

A big focus of this competency statement is on the required records for any distribution of a prescription drug. This includes records required for the distribution of controlled substances as discussed in Chapter 3. The recordkeeping requirements for the distribution of drugs also apply to a pharmacy when they are distributing drugs rather than dispensing drugs. A pharmacy may be engaged in the distribution of drugs when making a sale to a practitioner or to another pharmacy. For controlled substances, this can be done under the 5% rule as discussed in Chapter 3. Some states also have a 5% rule for all prescription drugs, not just controlled substances. This allows a pharmacy to make limited distributions, including sales to a practitioner's office, without having to be licensed as a drug wholesaler, although these laws may be preempted by the DSCSA. It is important to understand that pharmacies should not sell prescription drugs to practitioners by filling a prescription "for office use." Prescriptions generally must be issued for an individual person or animal. There may be exceptions in states for certain products, such as epinephrine auto-injectors, naloxone, or certain drugs to treat sexually transmitted diseases for which the prescriptions are not written for a specific person, but a practitioner writing a prescription "for office use" is not the legal way to make a sale to a practitioner's office.

4.2 Recordkeeping in compliance with legal requirements, including content, inventory, maintenance, storage, handling, and reporting:

Recordkeeping rules are always important on the MPJE. There are many laws that impact how long records are kept. It is best to concentrate on the recordkeeping requirements found in the state pharmacy practice act and rules, even if other laws may require you to keep the same records longer. For example, most states have rules on how long a pharmacy must maintain prescription records. These laws often require prescription records to be kept for 2–5 years. Other laws such as HIPAA or Medicaid and Medicare laws may have even longer recordkeeping requirements that cause a pharmacy to keep prescription records longer, but the MPJE should focus on the recordkeeping requirements under the pharmacy act and rules. In addition to prescription records, there may be different recordkeeping requirements for patient profiles or other records.

Even though nearly every pharmacy maintains records electronically, many of the recordkeeping rules were written before pharmacies used computers and before there were electronic prescriptions. Students often have difficulty understanding the manual recordkeeping rules because they are not really used in practice. Unfortunately, those rules are still in effect, and questions on them can show up on the MPJE exam. Specifically, you should know the requirements for filing prescription records. *See Chapter 3.* You should also review requirements for electronic recordkeeping, including any requirements for backing up systems.

4.2.1 Non-dispensing requirements for operations of pharmacies or practice settings

This competency statement previously specifically included topics such as space, equipment, advertising and signage, security (including temporary absences of the pharmacist), policies and procedures, libraries, required references, and the display of licenses. Most of these topics are self-explanatory. The security reference is important. As part of the security rules for pharmacies, most states require a pharmacist to be on duty when the pharmacy is open. This rule is most applicable to community pharmacy rules, but states may allow certain types of pharmacies to operate without a pharmacist present, including certain hospital pharmacies or other specialty practice pharmacies. Most states do not permit a pharmacy to be opened if a pharmacist does not show up to work. Pharmacy technicians and store managers would not be allowed to open a pharmacy if the pharmacist were not present. You should be familiar with the security rules for each type of pharmacy.

Be sure to review any rules regarding "temporary absence of the pharmacist" or "meal breaks." These rules allow a pharmacy to remain open while a pharmacist is on a break. They normally require the pharmacist to stay on the premises, but allow pharmacy technicians to remain in the pharmacy even though the pharmacist is on a break. You should understand what the pharmacy technicians can do in this situation, and how and if a patient may pick up a prescription while the pharmacist is on break.

Because this competency statement is about non-dispensing requirements, it may also include rules related to facilities such as remote order entry pharmacies or call-center pharmacies, where no drugs are stored or dispensed. You should be familiar with the basic requirements to operate these types of pharmacies. They often have less stringent security requirements and fewer requirements for specific types of equipment. They also often have a higher pharmacy technician to pharmacist ratio in states that still have such ratios.

4.2.2   Possession, storage, and handling of non-hazardous drugs

This competency statement is fairly broad. Although it is listed under statement 4.2, which is about recordkeeping, it is likely broader than that and may include questions about who may legally possess prescription drugs, and requirements related to drug handling and storage such as temperature requirements. The previous version of this statement listed topics such as investigational new drugs, repackaged or resold drugs, sample pharmaceuticals, recalls, and outdated pharmaceuticals. While it is unclear if these topics are still part of this competency, they are discussed below.

Investigational new drugs

Some states have detailed requirements on how pharmacies handle investigational drugs. Other states do not address this topic at all. There are comprehensive federal regulations on investigational drugs, but I would not expect those to be covered.

Repackaged or resold drugs

Chapter 2 includes a discussion about repackaging and makes it clear that a pharmacy may only repackage drugs for their own use. This is often called "prepackaging" to distinguish it from repackaging, which is considered FDA-regulated manufacturing.

Sample pharmaceuticals

See Chapter 2.

Recalls and outdated pharmaceuticals

See Chapter 2.

4.2.3 Training, possession, handling, storage, and disposal of hazardous drugs

This statement seems to be a reference to USP Chapter 800. *See Chapter 4 for discussion of USP Chapter 800.*

While USP Chapter 800 specifically addresses standards related to hazardous drugs, this competency statement may also encompass requirements of the Federal Hazard Communication Standard. This standard is administered and enforced by the Occupational and Safety Health Administration (OSHA). *See Chapter 2 for details.*

4.2.4 Allowing non-pharmacist personnel access to drugs

This competency statement is concerned with situations in which prescription drugs are either stored or sent to locations where there is not a pharmacist, and other situations where non-pharmacists are provided access to prescription drugs. It may include rules related to after-hours access to a pharmacy (including a hospital pharmacy), automated dispensing systems, drug kiosks, telepharmacies, and emergency kits in long-term care facilities.

After-hours access

You should look for any rules that allow non-pharmacists to access drugs "after hours" that are not stored in automated dispensing machines. Most states allow hospitals to adopt policies to permit physicians and/or nurses to access prescription drugs from a hospital pharmacy to meet the immediate needs of a patient when the pharmacy department is closed. These rules often require specific records, may limit the quantity of drugs that can be removed, and may require a pharmacist to review any drugs removed from the pharmacy within a certain period.

Automated dispensing systems

Automated dispensing machines such as Pyxis machines are used primarily in hospitals. They generally store unit-dose medications and medical supplies. They may also be used in other practice settings such as nursing homes, under some state laws. DEA allows their use in nursing homes as well, but a separate DEA registration for the automated machine is required since the controlled substances in the machine are not yet labeled for individual patients. The DEA number for the automated machine is issued to the pharmacy responsible for the machine but at the address of the nursing home. You should review rules for use of these automated dispensing machines in both hospitals and other locations, including rules related to where the machines may be located, who may restock the machines, who may access the machines, whether orders must be reviewed by a pharmacist prior to drugs being available for withdrawal from the machines, any overrides allowed whereby drugs can be accessed without pharmacist review, and whether the machines may be used for after-hours access to drugs when the pharmacy is closed.

Drug kiosks

Drug kiosks, or secure automated patient drug retrieval centers, allow patients to pick up or retrieve prescriptions that have already been dispensed. These are different from automated dispensing machines, which hold bulk drugs that have not yet been dispensed, such as a Pyxis machine in a hospital. These machines typically only store drugs that have already been dispensed by a pharmacy. The rules for these systems vary greatly from state to state. Some states do not allow them at all, others allow them only at the same location as the pharmacy or in medical facilities, and others allow them at any location approved by the Board of Pharmacy. Some states only allow them for refill medications, and others allow them for both new and refill prescriptions. They are often required to have audio/visual connections to the pharmacy to allow the pharmacist to counsel the patient if that is required in the state. DEA has not issued any rules or guidance on the use of these systems for controlled substance prescriptions. In the past, DEA has not allowed controlled substance prescriptions to be delivered to anyone other than the person to whom they were prescribed. For this reason, most states prohibit their use for controlled substances. Even if a state allows them to be used for controlled substances, it would be prudent to obtain some documentation from DEA that they permit this since they have not provided an opinion on these systems.

Telepharmacies

Telepharmacies include those locations using automated dispensing machines and remote dispensing sites that are staffed by a pharmacy technician. With either system, drugs are being dispensed and the dispensing is being supervised by a pharmacist at another location using audio/visual technology. Telepharmacy laws and rules are becoming much more prevalent in states. If your state has laws and rules relating to telepharmacies, you should be familiar with those requirements, including how patient counseling is provided and any restrictions. There are often restrictions on how far away the telepharmacy may be from the supervising pharmacy or from the nearest community pharmacy, the types of prescriptions that can be filled, the number of telepharmacy locations a pharmacist can manage, and how often a pharmacist must visit the telepharmacy site.

Emergency medication kits

Emergency medication kits in long-term care facilities are also an example of allowing non-pharmacist personnel access to prescription drugs. *See DEA Guidelines for Emergency Kits in Long-Term Care Facilities in Chapter 3.*

4.2.5   Requirements for conducting controlled substance inventories

See Chapter 3.

4.3   Delivery of drugs

This competency includes any rules related to the final step in the dispensing of a drug: the delivery to the patient. It could include rules related to the identification of the person accepting delivery of a drug, use of the mail or contract carriers for delivery, and drive-up windows. Drug kiosks rules may also fall under this competency, but those have been previously discussed under 4.2.4 above. Delivery rules may apply both to mail service pharmacies and community pharmacies that offer delivery services.

Identification

Some states may require an identification and/or signature of the person accepting delivery of prescription drugs, or may require this when prescription drugs are sent by mail. This is not a U.S. Postal Service regulation, nor is it required by DEA for controlled substances.

Mailing prescription drugs

Postal regulations permit drugs to be shipped by mail but do not permit mailing of alcoholic beverages, flammable substances, or poisons. Controlled substances may be sent by mail if the outer wrapper is free of markings that would indicate there are controlled substances inside. This means the name of the pharmacy should not appear as part of the return address, and the package may not be marked in any way to indicate the nature of the contents.

Some states have mail regulations or regulations for use of contract carriers that are more detailed and include things such as temperature monitoring or requirements for background checks of employees.

Drive-up windows

A few states have rules related to this topic. You should review any such rules in your state.

4.4   Conditions for permitted or mandated product selection

Generic substitution is such a widespread practice today that many students and pharmacists do not realize the history of substitution laws and how controversial they once were. It is estimated that 90% of all prescriptions dispensed are generic drugs, but the laws and rules on generic substitution can be complex and vary from state to state. Because this competency statement refers to "products," it includes both drugs and biological products. I will discuss generic drug substitution first and then discuss biological products.

Generic substitution

In general, the laws regarding generic substitution are much more likely to encourage substitution, or at least make refusing substitution difficult, because of the cost savings provided. Insurance companies and pharmacy benefit managers also want to reduce costs, so they may have rules regarding generic substitution that provide for lower co-pays for patients or other incentives to encourage substitution. But remember, the MPJE is not testing you on co-pays or insurance company reimbursement policies or dispensing rules, they are testing you on the state and federal laws. Because the government also pays for prescription drug coverage through Medicaid and Medicare, there may be laws on generic substitution specific to those programs in the pharmacy act or rules in some states, and those laws could be included on the MPJE.

Some states have mandatory generic substitution laws that require pharmacies to substitute a generic product if certain conditions are met. Most states have permissive substitution laws that permit the pharmacist to substitute a generic product if certain conditions are met. Even in permissive states, however, substitution may be mandatory for Medicaid or Medicare patients. In all states, one of the conditions that must be met is that the prescriber has not prohibited the substitution. You should be familiar with the specific requirements for a prescriber to prohibit substitution in your state. Many of these laws were written when most prescriptions were still issued as written prescriptions rather than electronic prescriptions, so they often have specific words that must be written on the prescription to prohibit substitution, such as "medically necessary," "brand medically necessary," or "dispense as written." Be sure to check and see if different rules apply to prohibit substitution on verbal or electronic prescriptions. Most states, but not all, also require that the patient provide consent or at least be notified of any substitution. Most states also require that the generic drug be less expensive than the brand name drug, and many also require that any cost savings be passed on to the patient.

States may also have positive and negative formularies. A positive formulary is a list of drugs that are considered generically equivalent and may be substituted, while a negative formulary is a list of drugs that are not considered equivalent and may not be substituted. Many states use the FDA Orange Book (*See Chapter 1*) as their positive formulary list, or they may require each pharmacy to develop their own positive formulary list and may only suggest pharmacies use the Orange Book to develop their positive formulary. A few states have a negative formulary that lists specific drugs that, by law, may not be substituted. If your state has a negative formulary, you should know the drugs on that list.

A few states have laws with restrictions on substituting certain drugs referred to as narrow therapeutic drugs. These may include drugs such as warfarin, carbamazepine, cyclosporine, digoxin, levothyroxine, lithium, phenytoin, and others. Other states have prohibitions on substituting certain categories of drugs such as anti-epileptic drugs or anti-arrhythmic agents. Be sure to be familiar with any such restrictions in your state.

Biological products

Most states have adopted biosimilar substitution laws for biological products. *See discussion of biosimilar products in Chapter 2.* Most state laws require that only biosimilar products that are designated as "interchangeable" may be substituted for the original reference product by a pharmacist. Like generic substitution laws, most state laws on biological substitution allow prescribers to block the substitution by indicating that the brand name product is medically necessary. They also often require that the pharmacist notify the prescriber of any substitution and that the substituted product be less expensive than the brand prescribed.

Change of dosage form and therapeutic substitution

Although no longer specifically mentioned in the competency statements, if your state has rules relating to a pharmacist's authority to change the dosage form of a prescription or to engage in therapeutic substitution (as opposed to generic substitution), those should be reviewed as well.

4.5　Compounding sterile, nonsterile, hazardous, and non-hazardous preparations

See Chapter 5 on USP Chapters 795, 797, and 800.

4.6　Centralized prescription processing or central fill pharmacy dispensing

Centralized processing

Centralized prescription processing is a method to reduce the workload of pharmacists at individual pharmacies. It involves having the processing functions in filling a prescription conducted at another pharmacy. These activities would include interpreting and clarifying prescriptions, data entry of the prescription into the pharmacy computer system, performing drug regimen review, obtaining refill and substitution authorizations, performing therapeutic interventions, and adjudicating the prescription claim. Unlike central fill, it does not include dispensing the prescription. The dispensing of the prescription is still conducted at the originating pharmacy, but the pharmacists and pharmacy technicians at that location do not have to do any of these processing activities. The processing activities are completed at the central processing pharmacy, and once they are completed, the prescription label is printed and the prescription is filled at the originating pharmacy. Although it is often called "central" or "centralized processing," some pharmacy chains do not centralize the processing of prescriptions to one location. They may just shift the processing functions from pharmacies that are very busy to pharmacies that are not as busy. This is sometimes called "workload balancing."

Notice that if a pharmacy is only performing central processing activities, they will not have any drugs in their pharmacy. Central processing may also include the processing of medication orders for hospital pharmacies depending on state law. This allows a hospital pharmacy to have medication orders reviewed by a pharmacist and entered in the hospital pharmacy computer system by a pharmacist at another pharmacy or hospital, usually during times the pharmacy department is closed. Some states have separate rules for hospitals and may refer to this as remote order processing. You should review the specific requirements for central processing pharmacies, including technology requirements, notifications to patients, labeling requirements, and any restrictions.

Central fill

Central fill involves one pharmacy preparing a prescription drug order for dispensing that has been transmitted to the central fill pharmacy by an originating pharmacy and returning the filled and labeled prescription to the originating pharmacy. The concept was first developed to relieve the workload in retail chain pharmacies, by having prescription refills that are often not picked up by the patient until the next day filled at a central fill facility rather than at the pharmacy where the patient would pick up the prescription. Central fill pharmacies are more efficient, as they are highly automated and can fill prescriptions for several pharmacies and then send those filled and labeled prescriptions to each originating pharmacy. Although central fill works best with refill prescriptions, some state rules allow it for original prescriptions as well. It is normally done amongst pharmacies that are under common ownership, but many state rules also allow pharmacies to contract with a central fill pharmacy.

DEA has modified their rules to allow central fill for controlled substance prescriptions and created a separate DEA registration for central fill pharmacies. Some states also allow central fill pharmacies to send the filled prescriptions directly to patients; however, it is important to note that DEA does not permit this for controlled substance prescriptions when the location is registered as a central fill pharmacy. DEA requires that a registered central fill pharmacy only delivers controlled substance prescriptions they prepare to the originating pharmacy.

You should review your state's requirements for a central fill pharmacy including technology, requirements, notifications to patients, labeling requirements, and any restrictions. Most states require that the originating pharmacy's name and phone number be placed on the label, as well as some type of identifier of the central fill pharmacy, such as the central fill pharmacy's DEA registration number or state license number. This is helpful in case there is an error; the board of pharmacy can determine which pharmacy filled the prescription. Some states require the name of the central fill pharmacy on the label and not just an identifier.

Remote order verification

Remote order verification is similar to central processing, but specifically allows a prescription or medication order to be reviewed and verified from a remote location. It may also be called "remote order entry" and, for hospital pharmacies, includes not just verification of a medication order, but also the entry of the order into the computer system. Remote verification may also include verifying the preparation or a prescription or medication order (often by a pharmacy technician) by a pharmacist from a remote location. This requires the use of some type of audio and visual technology that allows a pharmacist to see the product that was prepared. This could be considered a form of telepharmacy; however, telepharmacy is mentioned elsewhere in the competency statements, so this is more likely to involve order entry and verification activities and not a complete telepharmacy operation.

Central fill, central processing, and remote order entry are sometimes referred to as shared service operations in some states and may require specific licenses.

4.7   Requirements for the registration, licensure, certification, or permitting of a practice setting or business entity:

4.7.1   Requirements for registration, license, certification, or permitting of a practice setting

Just as competency statement 1.2 requires you to be familiar with the licensing of individuals, this competency statement requires you to know the licensing requirements for facilities. Pharmacy is unique amongst most other healthcare professions in that the state boards of pharmacy not only license the individuals who practice pharmacy, they also license the businesses or facilities. Boards of pharmacies may license many different types of facilities including in-state pharmacies, out-of-state pharmacies, specialty pharmacies, controlled substance registrants, wholesalers, distributors, manufacturers/repackagers, computer services providers, medical cannabis dispensaries, and internet pharmacies. Some state boards of pharmacy will not license all of these types of businesses. There may be another state agency that licenses facilities, such as wholesale distributors and manufacturers/repackagers. You should determine which agency in your state licenses these facilities. For the ones that are licensed by the board of pharmacy, be familiar with the requirements to obtain a license. Of particular note are out-of-state pharmacies. Nearly all states require pharmacies located out-of-state that ship or mail drugs to patients in the state to be licensed by the board of pharmacy. Many also require at least one pharmacist in the out-of-state pharmacy to be licensed in the state they are shipping to.

4.7.2   Requirements for the renewal or reinstatement of a license, registration, certificate, or permit of a practice setting

Pharmacy permits or licenses do not require continuing education requirements to be renewed, but you should review any specific requirements to renew a pharmacy permit.

4.7.3   Requirements for an inspection of a licensed, registered, certified, or permitted practice setting

Be sure you review the requirements for inspections of pharmacies, including whether an inspection is required before opening a pharmacy, how often pharmacies must be inspected, and any special inspections that must be done, such as for sterile compounding. Also, some states permit self-inspection of pharmacies. If your state allows for that, be sure to know the requirements for that program.

4.7.4 Classifications and processes of disciplinary actions that may be taken against a registered, licensed, certified, or permitted practice setting

This competency statement is similar to competency statement 1.2.2, on disciplinary processes and actions against individuals, but this one requires familiarity with the disciplinary process and types of disciplinary actions against pharmacies and other facility permits. Often, the process and types of disciplinary actions are similar to those against individuals, but you should make note of any differences.

CHAPTER TWO
Federal Food, Drug, and Cosmetic Act (FDCA), Poison Prevention Packaging Act (PPPA), and Other Miscellaneous Federal Laws

CHAPTER TWO
Federal Food, Drug, and Cosmetic Act (FDCA), Poison Prevention Packaging Act (PPPA), and Other Miscellaneous Federal Laws

I. **Federal Food, Drug, and Cosmetic Act (FDCA) and Major Amendments**
    A. Food, Drug, and Cosmetic Act of 1938
        1. Following deaths caused by sulfanilamide elixir in 1937, Congress passed the first legislation that required new drugs to be proven safe prior to marketing.
        2. Established the FDA and is the primary federal law dealing with food, drug, cosmetic, and medical device safety today (with many amendments).
    B. Durham-Humphrey Amendment of 1951
        1. Established two classes of drugs: prescription and over-the-counter (OTC).
        2. Authorized verbal prescriptions and prescription refills.

STUDY TIP: You are expected to know those pharmaceutical products that require a prescription. It is particularly important to know that certain products in the same drug class may be either prescription or nonprescription depending on the product or the strength. For example, some insulin products are nonprescription; however, certain other insulin products such as Lantus® and Humalog® are prescription-only products. Another example: ibuprofen products that are 400 mg, 600 mg, and 800 mg require a prescription, while ibuprofen 200 mg does not.

BONUS STUDY TIP: Dietary supplements and medical foods are both regulated by FDA as foods. They are not drugs. The MPJE competency statements do not mention these products, so they are not included in this review. However, medical foods seem to cause much confusion because they are intended to be consumed "under the direction of a physician." Despite this, FDA has made clear that they are not drugs and do not require a prescription. Some manufacturers incorrectly label some medical foods as "Rx only," but FDA has indicated that the use of "Rx only" on a medical food is misbranding.

C. Kefauver-Harris Amendments of 1962
  1. Required new drugs be proven safe and effective for their claimed use.
  2. Increased safety requirements for drugs and established Good Manufacturing Practices (GMPs) for manufacturing of drugs.
  3. Gave FDA jurisdiction over prescription drug advertising.

D. Prescription Drug Marketing Act of 1987 (PDMA)
  1. Bans the re-importation of prescription drugs and insulin products produced in the United States (except by the manufacturer).

     Note: The Medicine Equity and Drug Safety (MEDS) Act of 2000 and the Medicare Prescription Drug Improvement and Modernization Act of 2003 both have provisions that modified this part of the PDMA and allow importation of drugs under specific conditions. One of those conditions is that the Secretary of Health and Human Services (HHS) must certify to Congress that such imports do not threaten the health and safety of the American public and provide cost savings. On September 20, 2020, HHS finalized rules to allow importation of certain drugs from Canada. The rules permit states and Indian Tribes, and in certain future circumstances pharmacists and wholesalers, to submit importation program proposals to FDA for review and authorization. A few states have passed laws to allow drug importation from Canada and submitted proposals, but as of the date of publication of this book, no state plan has been approved by FDA.
  2. Prohibits the sale, trade, or purchase of prescription drug samples.
  3. Requires storage, handling, and recordkeeping requirements for prescription drug samples.
     a. These include obtaining written requests for samples from practitioners and requiring signatures of practitioners upon receipt.
     b. Samples may only be provided to practitioners, or to an institutional pharmacy or pharmacy of a healthcare entity upon request of a licensed practitioner that is affiliated with the healthcare facility.
     c. Community pharmacies should not possess prescription drug samples. One exception to this would be a community pharmacy that is part of a healthcare entity such as a community pharmacy owned by a hospital.

    4. Prohibits, with certain exceptions, the resale of prescription drugs purchased by hospitals or healthcare facilities and prescription drugs donated or sold at a reduced cost to charitable organizations.
Note: This is intended to prevent diversion of drugs due to price differences because hospitals generally receive lower prices for drugs than community pharmacies.

E. The Drug Quality and Security Act (DQSA) of 2013—These amendments to the FDCA addressed two primary topics: large-scale compounding by pharmacies and establishment of a framework for a uniform track-and-trace system for prescription drugs throughout the supply chain to prevent counterfeit drugs.

    1. Drug Compounding Quality Act (DCQA)

        a. Passed in response to an outbreak of fungal meningitis in over 20 states in the fall of 2012 that was traced to a contaminated injectable steroid produced by the New England Compounding Center. This outbreak resulted in the death of over 60 patients and over 750 cases of infection.

        b. Outsourcing facilities, often referred to as 503B facilities, are permitted to compound sterile products without receiving patient-specific prescriptions or medication orders. They are primarily regulated by FDA and are subject to FDA's current Good Manufacturing Practices (cGMPs).
Note: Despite this law being passed in 2013, there are currently only approximately 70 registered outsourcing facilities in the entire country.

c. Compounding pharmacies that are not registered with FDA as an "outsourcing facility" are often referred to as 503A facilities or 503A pharmacies and may only compound products pursuant to an individual prescription or medication order. They are permitted to do limited anticipatory compounding, are primarily regulated by the states, and are subject to USP quality standards for compounding.

d. Outsourcing facilities that meet the Act's requirements are exempt from the premarket approval requirements for new drugs (FDCA Section 505), adequate directions for use requirements (FDCA Section 502(f)(1)), and drug track-and-trace provisions (FDCA Section 582).
Note: Outsourcing facilities are not exempt from Good Manufacturing Practices.

STUDY TIP: Some states require all outsourcing facilities to be licensed as pharmacies. Other states license them as drug manufacturers. Check the rules in your state.

---

e. Outsourcing facilities must:
   (1) Have a licensed pharmacist who provides direct oversight over the drugs compounded;
   (2) Register as an outsourcing facility. The FDA website provides a list of the names of each outsourcing facility along with the state where the facility is located, whether the facility compounds from bulk drug substances, and whether drugs compounded from bulk are sterile or nonsterile;
   (3) Report to the Secretary of HHS upon registering, and every six months thereafter, the drugs sold in the previous six months;
   (4) Be inspected by FDA according to a risk-based inspection schedule and pay annual fees to support it;
   (5) Report serious adverse event experiences within 15 days and conduct a follow-up investigation and reporting similar to current drug manufacturers; and
   (6) Label products with a statement identifying them as a compounded drug and other specified information about the drug.

---

f. Outsourcing facilities may not compound a drug product that includes a bulk drug substance unless:

  (1) the bulk drug substance appears on a list identifying bulk drug substances for which there is a clinical need (the 503B bulks list); or

  (2) the drug product compounded from such bulk drug substance appears on FDA's drug shortage list at the time of compounding, distribution, and dispensing. *Note: Bulk drug substances must be accompanied by a valid certificate of analysis and must have been manufactured by an establishment registered with FDA. In addition, if an applicable United States Pharmacopeia (USP) or National Formulary monograph exists, bulk drug substances must comply with the monograph. FDA issued an Interim Policy on Compounding Using Bulk Drug Substances under Section 503B of the FDCA, which is in place while FDA develops the 503B bulks list. The guidance describes conditions under which the agency does not intend to take action against outsourcing facilities that compound drug products from bulk drug substances that cannot otherwise be used in compounding under Section 503B. See the compounding section of FDA's website for more information.*

g. Interstate distribution of compounded drugs from a 503A pharmacy.

  (1) Section 503A also limits interstate distribution of compounded drugs to 5% unless the compounder is located in a state that has entered into a memorandum of understanding (MOU) with FDA addressing inordinate amounts of compounded drugs in interstate commerce and providing for appropriate investigation of complaints by a state.

  (2) In states that have entered into an MOU with FDA, a pharmacy is considered to have distributed an inordinate amount of compounded drug products in interstate commerce if the number of prescription orders for compounded human drug products that the pharmacy distributed interstate during any calendar year is greater than 50% of the sum of:

(i) the number of prescription orders for compounded human drug products that the pharmacy sent out of (or caused to be sent out of) the facility in which the drug products were compounded during that same calendar year; plus

(ii) the number of prescription orders for compounded human drug products that were dispensed (e.g., picked up by a patient) at the pharmacy during that same calendar year.

Note: All of the compounded drugs must still be prepared based on an individually identified patient. Details on how these calculations are made can be found on the compounding page of FDA's website.

(3) In states that have not entered into an MOU with FDA, a pharmacy may not distribute (or cause to be distributed) compounded drug products out of the state in which they are compounded in quantities that exceed 5% of the total prescription orders dispensed or distributed by such pharmacy.

Note: FDA has announced that it is extending the period for states to decide whether to sign the MOU and before FDA begins enforcing the 5% rule. The new deadline for states to sign the MOU and comply with the 5% rule is October 22, 2022.

(4) FDA made a standard MOU available for states to sign in October 2020 that set forth obligations of states, including investigating complaints of adverse drug experiences and product quality issues for compounded products, identifying and investigating pharmacies distributing inordinate amounts of compounded drug products interstate, and required information sharing with FDA. The deadline for states to sign the MOU was extended until October 22, 2022, but a lawsuit filed by some compounding pharmacies has caused FDA to suspend the October 2020 MOU. FDA will now develop an MOU through the rulemaking process.

Note: FDA has issued several additional guidance documents to implement the Compounding Quality Act that are beyond the scope of this book. Detailed information may be found at FDA's website.

2. Drug Supply Chain Security Act (DSCSA) (Track and Trace)
   a. Provides for a uniform national framework for an electronic track-and-trace system for prescription drugs as they move through the supply chain and sets national standards for states to license drug wholesaler distributors.
   b. Applies to prescription drugs for human use in finished dosage form, but certain products are exempted, including blood and blood components, radioactive drugs, imaging drugs, certain intravenous products for fluid replacement, dialysis solutions, medical gases, compounded drugs, medical convenience kits containing drugs, certain combination products, sterile water, and products for irrigation.
   c. Manufacturers are required to provide "Transaction Data" for each product sold. Wholesalers are required to receive "Transaction Data" upon purchase and subsequently provide "Transaction Data" to buyer (pharmacies or other wholesalers), and pharmacies are required to receive transaction data and pass this information along if they further distribute the product.
   d. "Transaction Data" includes Transaction Information, Transaction History, and a Transaction Statement.
      (1) Transaction Information includes the product's name, strength, and dosage form; NDC number; container size and number of containers; date of transaction; and name and address of the person from whom ownership is being transferred and to whom ownership is being transferred. A unique product identifier or serialized numerical identifier (SNI) will also be required that identifies an individual bottle or unit of sale.
      (2) Transaction History is a paper or electronic statement that includes prior transaction information for each prior transaction back to the manufacturer.
      (3) Transaction Statement is a paper or electronic statement by the seller that the seller is authorized (licensed), received the product from an authorized (licensed) person, received the transaction information and transaction history from the prior owner if

required, did not knowingly ship a suspect or illegitimate product, has systems and processes to comply with verification requirements, and did not knowingly provide false transaction information.

STUDY TIP: Transaction Data must be maintained for 6 years by each supply chain partner.

---

e. Pharmacies may only receive drugs with product identifiers. Pharmacies are not yet required to authenticate (scan) those product identifiers.
Note: A product identifier is a standardized graphic with three elements: the product's standardized numerical identifier (SNI), which comprises the National Drug Code plus a unique alphanumeric serial number; a lot number; and an expiration date. Product identifiers must be in human- and machine-readable formats.

f. Pharmacies must investigate and properly handle suspect and illegitimate products.

(1) Suspect products are products that one has reason to believe are potentially counterfeit, diverted, stolen, subject to a fraudulent transaction, intentionally adulterated, or appear otherwise unfit for distribution such that they would result in serious adverse health consequences or death to humans.

(2) Illegitimate products are products for which credible evidence shows that the products are counterfeit, diverted, stolen, subject of a fraudulent transaction, intentionally adulterated, or appear otherwise unfit for distribution such that they would result in serious adverse health consequences or death to humans.

(3) Pharmacies must investigate any suspect or illegitimate product. As part of the investigation, a pharmacy must verify the product identifier of at least 3 products or 10% of the suspect product, whichever is greater, or all of the packages if there are fewer than 3. Pharmacies must also verify any illegitimate product in response to a notification of illegitimate product from FDA or a trading partner.

Note: This requirement was scheduled to go into effect on November 27, 2021, but FDA has delayed enforcement until November 27, 2023.

(4) If a product is illegitimate, pharmacies must notify FDA using Form FDA 3911 and notify trading partners within 24 hours. Pharmacies should also work with the manufacturer to prevent an illegitimate product from reaching patients.

g. Pharmacies that are "distributing" (distributing is defined as providing a drug to anyone other than the consumer/patient, as compared to dispensing, which is providing a drug to the patient/consumer) must have a wholesale distribution license and must pass DSCSA transaction data with that distribution. The only exceptions to having a distribution license and passing transaction data are as follows:

(1) When the distribution is between two entities that are affiliated or under common ownership;

(2) When a dispenser is providing product to another dispenser on a patient-specific basis;

(3) When a dispenser is distributing under emergency medical reasons; or

(4) When a dispenser is distributing "minimal quantities" to a licensed practitioner for office use.

h. The DSCSA also requires FDA to establish national standards for the licensure of wholesale drug distributors and third-party logistics providers. A third-party logistics provider, or 3PL, is an entity that provides or coordinates warehousing, or other logistics services of a product in interstate commerce on behalf of a manufacturer, wholesale distributor, or dispenser of a product, but does not take ownership of the product, nor have responsibility to direct the sale or disposition of the product. FDA issued a proposed rule for these licensure standards, which states may not change, on February 4, 2022, with enforcement to begin two years following finalization of the rule.

Note: FDA has issued more than 25 guidance documents on the DSCSA that are beyond the scope of this book, but can be found on FDA's DSCSA web page.

II. Prohibited Acts Under the FDCA

Nearly all violations of the FDCA cause the products to be adulterated and/or misbranded. It is important to understand the difference between these two concepts. Although drug manufacturers are more likely to violate the FDCA, actions taken by pharmacists (e.g., a dispensing error) could also cause a product to be adulterated or misbranded. It is likely these are the types of situations that may be covered on the MPJE.

A. Adulteration—A drug is adulterated if:

1. It contains any filthy, putrid, or decomposed substance.
2. It has been prepared or held under insanitary conditions where it may have been contaminated.
3. The methods of manufacture do not conform to current Good Manufacturing Practices (cGMPs).
4. It has been manufactured, processed, packed, or held in any factory, warehouse, or establishment and the owner, operator, or agent of such factory, warehouse, or establishment delays, denies, or limits an inspection, or refuses to permit entry or inspection.
5. The container is composed of any poisonous or deleterious substance which may contaminate the drug.
6. It contains an unsafe color additive.
7. It purports to be a drug in an official compendium and its strength differs from or its quality or purity falls below the compendium standard unless the difference is clearly stated on the label.
   Note: This means if the product claims to meet USP standards and its strength or quality does not meet those standards, it is adulterated.
8. It is not in a compendium, and its strength differs from or its quality falls below what it represents (i.e., what is on its label).
   Note: This means that even if the product does not claim to meet USP standards, if the strength or quality differs or falls below what is stated on its label or labeling, it is adulterated.

STUDY TIP: If a product's strength is less than what is represented on its label, it could be both misbranded and adulterated. *See C. below.*

---

9. It is mixed or packed with any substance that reduces its strength or quality, or the drug has been substituted in whole or in part.

B. Misbranding—A drug is misbranded if:
  1. The labeling is false or misleading in any particular way.
  2. It is a prescription drug and the manufacturer's labeling fails to contain the following information:
      a. The name and address of the manufacturer, packer, or distributor;
      b. Brand and/or generic name of the drug or drug product;
      c. The net quantity (weight, quantity, or dosage units);
      d. The weight of active ingredient per dosage unit;
      e. The federal legend, "Rx only";
      f. If not taken orally, the specific routes of administration (e.g., for IM injection);
      g. Special storage instructions, if appropriate;
      h. Manufacturer's control number (lot number);
      i. Expiration date; and
      j. Adequate information for use (package insert and Medication Guide or Patient Package Insert if required). This includes other information required (e.g., certain products, including opioids and benzodiazepines, require "black box warnings" to alert healthcare professionals about essential information regarding the product).

STUDY TIP: These labeling requirements are for the manufacturer's container. When a pharmacist dispenses a drug to a patient pursuant to a valid prescription, the label does not have to contain all these elements. State prescription labeling requirements would dictate what is required on the label.

---

  3. It is an OTC drug and fails to contain the following:
      a. A principal display panel, including a statement of identity of the product.
      b. The name and address of the manufacturer, packer, or distributor.
      c. Net quantity of contents.
      d. Cautions and warnings needed to protect user.
      e. Adequate directions for safe and effective use (for layperson).
      Note: OTC products must have adequate directions for safe and effective use, while prescription products must have adequate information for use (i.e., the package insert).

    f. Content and format of OTC product labeling in "Drug Facts" panel format, including:
      (1) Active Ingredients.
      (2) Purpose.
      (3) Use(s)—indications.
      (4) Warnings.
      (5) Directions.
      (6) Other Information.
      (7) Inactive Ingredients (in alphabetical order).
      (8) Questions? (optional), followed by telephone number.

STUDY TIP: Pharmacists do not usually concern themselves with the OTC labeling requirements in 3. above, as it is expected that manufacturers will label their products appropriately; but you should know the labeling requirements for OTC drugs for the MPJE.

---

    4. It is a drug liable to deterioration unless it is packaged or labeled accordingly.
    5. The container is made, formed, or filled as to be misleading.
    6. The drug is an exact imitation of another drug or offered for sale under the name of another drug.
    7. It is dangerous to health when used in the dosage or manner suggested in the labeling.
    8. It is packaged or labeled in violation of the Poison Prevention Packaging Act.

STUDY TIP: The FDCA specifically states that a drug that is not packaged in a child-resistant container (if required) is misbranded. This may not be as obvious because it is about the packaging and not the label or labeling.

---

    9. If it was manufactured, prepared, propagated, compounded, or processed in an establishment not registered by FDA or the product is not listed with FDA.
  C. Adulteration and Misbranding as Applied to Pharmacies
    1. Dispensing a prescription without authorization causes the drug to be misbranded even if it is labeled correctly by the pharmacist. This is because a prescription drug product is only exempt from the manufacturer's labeling requirements in B.2. above when it is dispensed pursuant to a valid prescription.

2. Misfilling a prescription with the wrong drug, strength, or directions for use will always cause the drug to be misbranded.

3. If a misfilled prescription involves the wrong strength of the drug prescribed, it would also be adulterated. This is because the definition of adulteration includes when the strength differs from or quality falls below that which it represents.

4. If a drug is subject to a Risk Evaluation and Mitigation Strategy (REMS) and it is prescribed or dispensed without meeting the requirements of the REMS, it is misbranded because the REMS program is part of the official labeling of the drug.

5. The advertising or promotion of a compounded drug that is false or misleading would be misbranding.

6. An expired drug product in a manufacturer's bottle is adulterated because after the expiration date, the strength cannot be assured. If a prescription is filled using an expired product, it may also be misbranded if the pharmacist placed a beyond-use date that is after the expiration date of the drug.

7. If a pharmacist counts a medication on a tray that has residue from another medication, the product would be adulterated.

8. If a pharmacist stores inventory in a room or refrigerator where the temperature is not adequately controlled, the products would be adulterated.

9. If a pharmacist stores a specific product incorrectly, such as stocking a medication on a pharmacy shelf instead of in the refrigerator as required, this will lead to the product being adulterated.

10. If a pharmacist fails to dispense a medication in a child-resistant container when required, this would be misbranding.

III. Other Provisions of the FDCA and Federal Regulations
A. Special Warning Requirements for OTC Products in the FDCA

STUDY TIP: These are special labeling requirements under federal regulations for products containing these ingredients or for specific drug categories. Normally the manufacturer's label would include these warnings, but you should be familiar with these requirements.

1. FD&C Yellow No. 5 (tartrazine) and No. 6 (21 CFR 201.20)—Must disclose presence and provide warning in "precautions" section of label that may cause allergic reaction in certain susceptible persons.
2. Aspartame (21 CFR 201.21)—Must contain warning in "precautions" section of labeling to the following effect: Phenylketonurics: Contains phenylalanine __ mg per (dosage unit).
3. Sulfites (21 CFR 201.22)—Prescription drugs containing sulfites (often used as a preservative) must contain an allergy warning in the "warnings" section of the labeling.
4. Mineral Oil (21 CFR 201.302)—Requires warning to only be taken at bedtime and not be used in infants unless under advice of a physician. Label also cannot encourage use during pregnancy.
5. Wintergreen Oil (methyl salicylate) (21 CFR 201.303 and 201.314(g)(1))—Any drug containing more than 5% methyl salicylate (often used as flavoring agent) must include warning that any use other than directed may be dangerous and that the article should be kept out of reach of children.
6. Sodium Phosphates (21 CFR 201.307)—Limits the amount of sodium phosphates oral solution to not more than 90 ml per OTC container. Also requires specific warnings.
7. Isoproterenol inhalation preparations (21 CFR 201.305)—Requires warning not to exceed dose prescribed and to contact physician if difficulty in breathing persists.
8. Potassium Salt Preparations for Oral Ingestions (21 CFR 201.306)—Requires warning regarding nonspecific small-bowel lesions consisting of stenosis, with or without ulceration, associated with the administration of enteric-coated thiazides with potassium salts.
9. Ipecac Syrup (21 CFR 201.308)
    a. The following statement (boxed and in red letters) must appear: "For emergency use to cause vomiting in

poisoning. Before using, call physician, the poison prevention center, or hospital emergency room immediately for advice."

    b. The following warning must appear: "Warning: Keep out of reach of children. Do not use in unconscious persons."

    c. The dosage of the medication must appear. The usual dosage is 1 tablespoon (15 ml) in individuals over 1 year of age.

    d. May only be sold in 1 oz. (30 ml) containers.

10. Phenacetin (acetophenetidin) (21 CFR 201.309)—Must contain warning about possible kidney damage when taken in large amounts or for a long period of time.

11. Salicylates (21 CFR 201.314)—Aspirin and other salicylate drugs must have special warnings for use in children including warning regarding Reye's syndrome. Retail containers of 1¼ grain (pediatric) aspirin cannot be sold in containers holding more than 36 tablets.

12. OTC Drugs for Minor Sore Throats (21 CFR 201.315)—Any OTC product that states "For the temporary relief of minor sore throats" must include this warning:
"Warning—Severe or persistent sore throat or sore throat accompanied by high fever, headache, nausea, and vomiting may be serious. Consult physician promptly. Do not use more than 2 days or administer to children under 3 years of age unless directed by physician."

13. Alcohol Warning (21 CFR 201.322)—Internal analgesics and antipyretics including acetaminophen, aspirin, ibuprofen, naproxen, ketoprofen, etc., are required to have a warning for persons consuming 3 or more alcoholic beverages per day and to consult with a doctor before taking.

14. Over-the-counter drugs for vaginal contraceptive and spermicide use containing nonoxynol 9 as the active ingredient (21 CFR 201.325)—Are subject to several warning requirements, including one that states, "Sexually transmitted diseases (STDs) alert: This product does not protect against HIV/AIDS or other STDs and may increase the risk of getting HIV from an infected partner."

15. OTC Pain Relievers (21 CFR 201.326)

    a. Acetaminophen.

        (1) Must have "acetaminophen" prominently displayed.

        (2) Must warn about liver toxicity.

      (3) Must warn not to use with other products containing acetaminophen and to talk to a doctor or pharmacist before taking with warfarin.

   b. Nonsteroidal Anti-inflammatory Drugs (NSAIDs).

      (1) Must include term "NSAID" prominently on label.

      (2) Must contain "stomach bleeding" warning.

16. OTC Products Containing Iron in Solid Oral Dosage Form (21 CFR 310.518(a))

   a. Must provide the following warning: "Accidental overdose of iron-containing products is a leading cause of fatal poisoning in children under 6. Keep this product out of reach of children. In case of accidental overdose, call a doctor or poison control center immediately."

   b. This warning requirement also applies to dietary supplements containing iron through 21 CFR 101.17(e).

   c. FDA previously had a rule that required unit-dose packaging for iron-containing dietary supplements and drug products that contain 30 milligrams (mg) or more of iron per dosage unit, but that rule was eliminated based on a court case in 2003 that concluded FDA did not have the authority to pass such a rule.

B. Additional OTC Requirements

  1. Tamper-Evident Packaging

   a. Manufacturers and packagers of OTC drugs for sale at retail must package OTC products in tamper-evident packaging.

   b. Certain products are exempted, including dermatologicals, dentifrices (e.g., toothpaste), insulins, and lozenges.

   c. OTC products not packaged in tamper-resistant packaging would be considered adulterated and misbranded.

STUDY TIP: FDA regulations state that an OTC drug product (except a dermatological, dentifrice, insulin, or lozenge product) for retail sale that is not packaged in a tamper-resistant package or that is not properly labeled as required under the tamper-evident requirements is adulterated or misbranded, or both. It is likely both because if the packaging is not tamper-evident, it is adulterated because the definition of adulteration says that the product is packed whereby it "may" have been contaminated or rendered injurious to health. It is also misbranded because the product does not meet the packaging requirements.

---

2. Repackaging of OTC Products—A pharmacist that repackages OTC products would be subject to cGMP requirements and would have to meet all additional requirements including the manufacturer labeling and tamper-evident packaging if offered for sale to the public.

STUDY TIP: If a patient wishes to purchase an OTC drug in a smaller package size than what is commercially available, a pharmacist cannot break open a commercial OTC product and sell the lesser quantity by placing it in a vial and labeling it. The only way this can be done is if the patient has a prescription for the smaller quantity and the OTC drug is filled as a prescription as discussed below.

---

3. When an OTC product is prescribed and filled as a prescription, the OTC labeling requirements do not have to be followed. The prescription drug labeling requirements would apply and would include the prescriber's directions for use. If an OTC drug is filled as a prescription, any instructions for refills would apply as would beyond-use dates required for prescription drugs.
C. FDA Drug and Device Recall Classifications
  1. Class I—Reasonable probability product will cause either serious adverse effects on health or death.
  2. Class II—May cause temporary or medically reversible adverse effects on health or where probability of serious adverse effects is remote.
  3. Class III—Not likely to cause adverse health consequences.
D. Advertising and Promotion of Prescription Drugs
  1. Prescription drug advertising is regulated by FDA.
  2. Over-the-counter (OTC) drug advertising is regulated by the Federal Trade Commission (FTC).
  3. Advertising of Prescription Drug Prices (including by pharmacists)—The advertising of prescription drug prices is considered reminder advertising under FDA regulations (21 CFR 200.200). However, such advertising is exempt from FDA advertising regulations provided that the following conditions are met:
    a. The only purpose of the advertising is to provide information on price, not information on the drug's safety, efficacy, or indications for use.

        b. The advertising contains the proprietary name of the drug (if any), the generic name of the drug, the drug's strength, the dosage form, and the price charged for a specific quantity of the drug.

        c. The advertising may include other information, such as the availability of professional or other types of services, as long as it is not misleading.

        d. The price stated in the advertising shall include all charges to the consumer; mailing and delivery fees, if any, may be stated separately.

    4. A pharmacy that compounds products may advertise that they provide compounding services, including that they compound specific products. However, if a pharmacy makes any therapeutic claims regarding those products, they would be subject to FDA's rules on advertising, which are complex and beyond the scope of this book.

E. Patient Package Inserts (PPIs)

    1. Supplied by the manufacturer and written for a layperson.

    2. Required to be given to patients in the community setting when new and refill prescriptions for certain products are dispensed.

    3. Currently required for:

        a. Oral contraceptives (21 CFR 310.501).

        b. Estrogen-containing products (21 CFR 310.515).

    4. Hospitalized or institutionalized patients—A PPI must also be provided to a patient prior to the first administration of the drug and every 30 days thereafter.

STUDY TIP: This is a good example of something that may not happen in practice, but you need to know it is technically required.

---

    5. Failure to provide a PPI for these drugs would cause them to be misbranded.

F. Medication Guides (MedGuides)

    1. Similar to PPI program but with amended requirements for institutionalized patients.

    2. FDA requires Medication Guides for all new and refill prescriptions dispensed in the community setting when:

        a. Patient labeling could prevent serious adverse effects.

        b. Product has serious risks relative to benefits.

        c. Patient adherence to directions is crucial.

3. Medication Guides must be written in a standard format and in language suitable for patients.
4. Manufacturers must obtain FDA approval before distributing Medication Guides and are responsible for ensuring that a sufficient number of Medication Guides are provided to pharmacies. Many manufacturers include the Medication Guide at the bottom of the package insert, but most pharmacy computer systems also print Medication Guides for the products that need them at the time of dispensing.
5. FDA maintains a searchable Medication Guide database on its website, and there are hundreds of products that now require a Medication Guide. Some of the drugs, drug classes, and biologicals requiring Medication Guides include:
   a. Accutane® (isotretinoin).
   b. Antidepressants in children and teenagers.
   c. Coumadin® (warfarin sodium).
   d. Epogen® (epoetin alfa).
   e. Forteo® (teriparatide, rDNA origin).
   f. Lindane® shampoo and lotion.
   g. Lotronex® (alosetron hydrochloride).
   h. Nolvadex® (tamoxifen).
   i. Non-Steroidal Anti-Inflammatory Drugs (NSAIDs).
   j. Remicade® (infliximab).
   k. Trizivir® (abacavir sulfate, lamivudine, and zidovudine).
   l. Opioid analgesics and cough products.
      Note: In 2022, FDA sought public comments on modifying the REMS for opioid analgesics to require that mail-back envelopes be dispensed and education on safe disposal be provided with opioid analgesics dispensed in an outpatient setting. This was not finalized at the time of publication of this book but could become a requirement if implemented.
   m. Benzodiazepines.
6. Failure to provide a Medication Guide when dispensing a drug that requires one would cause the drug to be misbranded.

STUDY TIP: Consumer Medication Information (CMI), which is often provided to community pharmacy patients for all new and refill prescriptions dispensed, is written patient information that is not equivalent to or substitutable for FDA regulated and mandated PPIs and MedGuides.

G. Prescription Drugs: Side Effects Statement
1. To enable consumers to report side effects of prescription drugs to FDA, pharmacies and pharmacists are required to distribute a side effects statement to patients when dispensing all new and refill prescriptions in the outpatient setting.
2. The side effects statement provided with each prescription drug must read: "Call your doctor for medical advice about side effects. You may report side effects to FDA at 1-800-FDA-1088."
3. The side effects statement can be distributed on a sticker attached to the pharmacy container, on a preprinted pharmacy prescription vial cap, or on a separate sheet of paper, or found within CMI or MedGuides.

H. Risk Evaluation and Mitigation Strategies (REMS)
1. REMS are strategies to manage a known or potential serious risk associated with a drug, drug class, or biological product. FDA requires a REMS if FDA finds that it is necessary to ensure that the benefits of the drug, drug class, or biological product outweigh the risks of the product. A REMS can include a Medication Guide, Patient Package Insert, a communication plan, elements to assure safe use, and an implementation system. It must also include a timetable for assessment of the REMS.
2. Elements to assure safe use may include:
   a. Special training, experience, or certification of healthcare practitioners prescribing the drugs;
   b. Special certification for pharmacies, practitioners, or healthcare settings that dispense the drugs;
   c. Dispensing drugs to patients only in certain healthcare settings such as hospitals;
   d. Dispensing drugs to patients with evidence or other documentation of safe use conditions, such as laboratory test results;
   e. Monitoring patients using the drugs; or
   f. Enrolling each patient using the drug in a registry.
3. A complete list of products with approved REMS can be found on FDA's website and may include an entire drug class such as the Opioid Analgesic REMS. Below are summaries of two of the most extensive REMS, but you should be familiar with the most common REMS and which products are subject to REMS.

4. Example REMS—Isotretinoin (Accutane) iPLEDGE Program
   a. Only doctors registered in iPLEDGE can prescribe isotretinoin. Doctors registered with iPLEDGE must agree to assume the responsibility for pregnancy counseling of female patients of childbearing potential. Prescribers must obtain and enter into the iPLEDGE system negative test results for those female patients of childbearing potential prior to prescribing isotretinoin.
   b. Only patients registered in iPLEDGE can be prescribed isotretinoin. In addition to registering with iPLEDGE, patients must comply with a number of key requirements that include completing an informed consent form, obtaining counseling about the risks and requirements for safe use of the drug, and, for women of childbearing potential, complying with required pregnancy testing and use of contraception.
   c. Only pharmacies registered in iPLEDGE can dispense isotretinoin. To register in iPLEDGE, a pharmacy must select a Responsible Site Pharmacist who must obtain iPLEDGE program information and registration materials via the internet (*www.ipledgeprogram.com*) or telephone (1-866-495-0654) and sign and return the completed registration form. To activate registration, the Responsible Site Pharmacist must access the iPLEDGE program via the internet (*www.ipledgeprogram.com*) or telephone (1-866-495-0654) and attest to the following points:
      (1) I know the risk and severity of fetal injury/birth defects from isotretinoin.
      (2) I will train all pharmacists on the iPLEDGE program requirements.
      (3) I will comply and seek to ensure that all pharmacists comply with iPLEDGE program requirements.
      (4) I will obtain isotretinoin from iPLEDGE-registered wholesalers.
      (5) I will return to the manufacturer (or delegate) any unused product.
      (6) I will not fill isotretinoin for any party other than a qualified patient.

    d. To dispense isotretinoin, pharmacists must obtain a Risk Management Authorization (RMA) from iPLEDGE via the internet (*www.ipledgeprogram.com*) or telephone (1-866-495-0654), signifying the patient is registered, has received counseling and education, and is not pregnant.

    e. Product is dispensed in blister packages which cannot be broken, and a 30-day supply is the maximum quantity that can be dispensed.

    f. No refills are allowed.

5. Example REMS—Thalomid (Thalidomide) REMS

    a. Prescriber Requirements

      (1) The prescriber enrolls and becomes certified with Celgene for the Thalomid REMS program.

      (2) The prescriber counsels patient on benefits and risks of Thalomid.

      (3) The prescriber provides contraception and emergency contraception counseling.

      (4) The prescriber verifies negative pregnancy test for all female patients of reproductive potential.

      (5) The prescriber completes a Thalomid Patient-Physician Agreement Form with each patient and sends to Celgene.

      (6) The prescriber/patient completes applicable mandatory confidential survey.

      (7) The prescriber obtains an authorization number from Celgene and writes it on every prescription along with patient risk category.

      (8) The prescriber writes no more than a 4-week (28-day) supply, with no automatic refills or telephone prescriptions.

      (9) The prescriber sends Thalomid prescription to certified pharmacy.

    b. Pharmacy Requirements

      (1) Pharmacy must be certified in the Thalomid REMs program with Celgene.

      (2) Prescriptions can only be accepted with an authorization number and patient risk category.

      (3) Authorization numbers are valid for 7 days from the date of the last pregnancy test for females of reproductive potential and 30 days from the date issued for other patients.

(4) Pharmacy must obtain a confirmation number prior to dispensing via toll-free number or online. The confirmation number is valid for 24 hours and must be entered on the prescription. This means the prescription must be dispensed within 24 hours of obtaining the confirmation number.

(5) No automatic refills or telephone prescriptions are permitted.

(6) Prescription must be written for a 4-week (28 day) supply or less.

(7) No refills are allowed, and subsequent prescriptions may be dispensed only if there are 7 days or less remaining on the existing prescription.

(8) A certified Thalomid REMS counselor must counsel the patient, and counseling must be documented.

(9) Prescription must be dispensed with a medication guide.

(10) Prescriptions cannot be transferred to another pharmacy without prior authorization from Celgene.

I. National Drug Code (NDC) Number

1. A unique 10- or 11-character number that identifies a drug by manufacturer or packager (labeler), product, and package size. NDC numbers will have one of the following configurations: 4-4-2, 5-3-2, or 5-4-1.

a. First 4 to 5 digits = labeler code.

b. Next 3 to 4 digits = specific drug, strength, dosage form.

c. Last 1 to 2 digits = package size.

2. NDC numbers are required for a drug manufacturer to list their product with FDA, and FDA suggests they be included on the drug's label, but it is not technically required. All drug manufacturers include an NDC number because they facilitate automated processing of drug data by government agencies, third-party payers, wholesalers, and manufacturers.

STUDY TIP: NDC numbers should not appear on non-drug products. If a dietary supplement or medical device has an NDC number on its label, it would be misbranded. Medical devices have unique device identifiers (UDIs) instead of NDC numbers. Any product that implies it is an FDA-approved drug and it is not would also be misbranded.

---

3. While nearly all drug products have an NDC number, an NDC code does not indicate a drug is approved by FDA. There are some unapproved drugs that have NDC numbers.

4. Although the NDC is 10 digits, the standard for billing and claims submissions is an 11-digit NDC. This is accomplished by inserting a leading zero into one of the segments: first segment if it is four numbers, second segment if it is three numbers, or added to the beginning of the third segment if it only has one number.

5. On July 25, 2022, FDA published a proposed rule to change the NDC to 12 digits in length, with three distinct and consistent segments and one uniform format. This rule is only proposed, and even when finalized there will be a transition period before it is fully implemented.

J. FDA Orange Book
1. Official name is *Approved Drug Products with Therapeutic Equivalence Evaluations.*
2. Available at *http://www.fda.gov/cder/ob/.*
3. The primary source for determining generic equivalency of drugs. To be considered generically equivalent, a drug must be both pharmaceutically equivalent and therapeutically equivalent to the reference drug product (normally the brand-name drug).
4. Definitions
   a. Pharmaceutical equivalents are drug products in identical dosage forms and route(s) of administration that contain identical amounts of the identical active drug ingredient.
   b. Therapeutic equivalents are approved drug products that are pharmaceutical equivalents for which bioequivalence has been demonstrated, and they can be expected to have the same clinical effect and safety profile when administered to patients under the conditions specified in the labeling.
   Note: This means the drug is bioequivalent to the reference drug product.
5. Uses 2-letter coding system to indicate equivalency with first letter being the key:
   a. A = Drug products that FDA considers to be pharmaceutically equivalent and therapeutically equivalent.

    b. B = Drug products that FDA considers NOT to be pharmaceutically equivalent and therapeutically equivalent.

STUDY TIP: The first letter of the 2-letter code tells you if the product is considered equivalent. It is recommended that the reader look up an Orange Book listing in the FDA Orange Book database online and be familiar with format.

---

    6. Products with no known or suspected bioequivalence issues:
        a. AA—conventional dosage forms.
        b. AN—solutions and powders for aerosolization.
        c. AO—injectable oil solutions.
        d. AP—injectable aqueous solutions.
        e. AT—topical products.
    7. Products with actual or potential bioequivalence problems, but for which adequate scientific evidence has established bioequivalence for those products, are given a rating of AB.
    8. There are situations where there may be multiple pharmaceutically equivalent reference drugs that have not been determined to be bioequivalent to each other. For these products, FDA implemented a 3-character code such as AB1, AB2, and AB3. If a generic drug product establishes bioequivalence to one of the reference drugs, it will receive the same 3-character code as the reference drug. An example includes Adalat CC (AB1) and Procardia XL (AB2). Both are reference drugs with the same dosage form and active ingredients, but they are not rated as bioequivalent to each other.
K. FDA Purple Book
    1. Official name is *Lists of Licensed Biological Products with Reference Product Exclusivity and Biosimilarity or Interchangeability Evaluations*.
    2. Lists biological products that are considered biosimilars and provides interchangeability evaluations for these products.
    3. Biosimilar or biosimilarity means that the biological product is highly similar to the reference product notwithstanding minor differences in clinically inactive components, and there are no clinically meaningful differences between the biological product and the reference product in terms of the safety, purity, and potency of the product.
    4. An interchangeable product is a product that has been shown to be biosimilar to the reference product and can be

expected to produce the same clinical result as the reference product in any given patient.

5. Only biological products that have been designated "interchangeable" may be substituted for the original reference product by a pharmacist. Biosimilar products would require prescriber intervention in order to substitute.

    Note: While there are several biosimilar products on the market (such as adalimumab, bevacizumab, and epoetin alfa), FDA has only designated a few of them as interchangeable. The first interchangeable biological was approved by FDA in July 2021 when Semglee (insulin glargine-yfgn) was designated by FDA as interchangeable with (can be substituted at the pharmacy level for) its reference product Lantus® (insulin glargine).

STUDY TIP: The FDA Orange Book and Purple Book are federal references that guide healthcare professionals in evaluating the substitution of approved drug products and biologics. States may adopt these references as law; the states that do this are often termed Orange Book and/or Purple Book states.

L. Medical Devices

1. FDA regulates companies that manufacture and repackage medical devices.

2. A medical device includes instruments, apparatuses, machines, implants, or other related articles intended to treat or prevent disease but, unlike drugs, does not achieve its primary purpose through chemical action within or on the body and does not depend on being metabolized.

3. FDA classifies medical devices based on the risk association with the device.

    a. Class I devices are deemed to be low risk and are therefore subject to the least regulatory controls. Dental floss is an example.

    b. Class II devices are higher risk and require greater regulatory controls. Syringes are an example.

    c. Class III devices are subject to the highest level of regulatory control, and those that pose a significant risk of illness or injury require premarket approval by FDA. Replacement heart valves are an example.

4. Not all medical devices require a prescription, but many do (e.g., contact lenses).

5. Certain Class I and Class II devices are exempt from pre-market approval and GMPs but typically must still comply with other regulatory requirements unless they are exempt.

M. Animal Drugs
   1. FDA regulates drugs intended to be used by animals.
   2. Animal drugs have to be approved by FDA as safe and effective.
   3. FDA determines if an animal drug can be sold as a prescription or OTC.
   4. Animal prescription products can be dispensed only by or upon the lawful written order of a licensed veterinarian.
   5. The manufacturer's label of an animal prescription drug product must bear the legend: "Caution: Federal law restricts this drug to use by or on the order of a licensed veterinarian."
   6. Veterinarians can also legally prescribe approved human drugs for animals in certain circumstances (this is called extra-label or off-label use). Therefore, pharmacies and pharmacists may receive and dispense such prescriptions.
   7. FDA has also released guidance regarding the compounding of animal drugs, which pharmacies may participate in.

N. Emergency Contraception (Plan B)
   1. When single pill levonorgestrel (Plan B One-Step) was first made available without a prescription, it had age restrictions. It was initially only available without a prescription for women age 17 and older. There was also confusion, political controversy, and lawsuits surrounding the age limitations for Plan B One-Step that are beyond the scope of this book.
   2. Since 2013, Plan B One-Step, and similar generic versions of single dose levonorgestrel, are available without a prescription to anyone, of any age. These products are often still kept behind the counter.
   3. Next Choice, the two-pill emergency contraceptive option, does have an age restriction. It is available behind the counter without a prescription for women 17 and older. Women under 17 still need a prescription.
   4. No states currently restrict the sale of Plan B, but given the overturning of *Roe v. Wade* in *Dobbs vs. Jackson Women's Health Organization*, new legislation may be introduced to do so in some states, and there may be legislation to strengthen or expand access in other states.

IV. Poison Prevention Packaging Act of 1970 (PPPA)

    A. Administered by Consumer Product Safety Commission (CPSC).

    B. Requires child-resistant containers for all prescriptions and for the following nonprescription drugs, drug classes, preparations, or dietary supplements:

        1. Aspirin—Any aspirin-containing preparation for human use in dosage form intended for oral administration.

        2. Methyl salicylate (oil of wintergreen)—Liquid preparations containing more than 5% by weight of methyl salicylate unless packaged in pressurized spray containers.

        3. Controlled drugs—Any preparation for human use in a dosage form intended for oral administration that consists in whole or in part of any substance subject to control under the Federal Controlled Substances Act.
Note: There are some Schedule V controlled substances available without a prescription under federal law. See Chapter 3.

        4. Methyl alcohol (methanol)—Household substances in liquid form containing 4% or more by weight of methyl alcohol unless packaged in a pressurized spray container.

        5. Iron-containing drugs—With the exception of animal feeds used as vehicles for the administration of drugs, noninjectable animal and human drugs providing iron for therapeutic or prophylactic purposes, which contain a total amount of elemental iron equivalent to 250 mg.

        6. Dietary supplements containing iron—With the exception of those preparations in which iron is present solely as a colorant, dietary supplements that contain an equivalent of 250 mg or more of elemental iron in a single package.

        7. Acetaminophen—Preparations for human use in a dosage form intended for oral administration and containing more than 1 g of acetaminophen in a single package.
Exemptions:

            a. Acetaminophen-containing effervescent tablets or granules containing less than 10% acetaminophen with a median lethal dose greater than 5 g/kg of body weight and that release at least 85 ml of carbon dioxide per grain of acetaminophen when placed in water.

            b. Unflavored acetaminophen-containing preparations in powder form, other than those intended for pediatric use, that are packaged in unit doses with no more than 13 grains of acetaminophen per unit dose and that contain no other substance subject to the special packaging requirements.

8. Diphenhydramine HCl—Preparations for human use in oral dosage forms containing more than the equivalent of 66 mg of diphenhydramine base in a single package.

9. Ibuprofen—Preparations for human use in oral dosage forms containing 1 gram or more of ibuprofen in a single package.

10. Loperamide—Preparations for human use in oral dosage forms containing more than 0.045 mg of loperamide in a single package.

11. Lidocaine—Products containing more than 5 mg of lidocaine in a single package (includes all dosage forms including creams, sprays, and transdermal patches).

12. Dibucaine—Products containing more than 0.5 mg of dibucaine in a single package (includes all dosage forms including creams, sprays, and transdermal patches).

13. Naproxen—Preparations for human use in oral dosage forms containing 250 mg or more of naproxen in a single package.

14. Ketoprofen—Preparations for human use in oral dosage forms containing more than 50 mg of ketoprofen in a single package.

15. Fluoride—Products containing more than 50 mg of elemental fluoride and more than 0.5% fluoride in a single package.

16. Minoxidil—Preparations for human use containing more than 14 mg of minoxidil in a single package (includes topical products that must continue to meet requirements once applicator is installed by consumer).

17. Imidazolines—Products containing 0.08 mg or more in a single package. Imidazolines include tetrahydrozoline, naphazoline, oxymetazoline, and xylometazoline and are often found in ophthalmic and nasal products.

18. Any drug switched from Rx to OTC status.

C. Exemptions:

1. Request of patient or physician.

STUDY TIP: Only the patient can provide a blanket request for all future prescriptions. The prescriber can only request a non-child-resistant container on an individual prescription. The request is not legally required to be in writing, although it is good practice to have it in writing.

---

2. Bulk containers not intended for household use.
3. Drugs distributed to institutionalized patients, including hospitalized patients or residents of LTCFs and other institutional settings if facility personnel will administer the medications to the patients.

STUDY TIP: Would a prescription dispensed to a patient in an assisted-living facility be exempt from the child-resistant container requirements? Only if the drugs are administered by facility personnel or another exemption applies, such as request of the patient.

---

4. One package size of OTC drugs designed for the elderly.
5. Specific prescription and nonprescription drug exemptions include:
   a. Oral contraceptives, conjugated estrogens, and norethindrone acetate in manufacturer's dispenser package.
   b. Medroxyprogesterone acetate tablets.
   c. Sublingual nitroglycerin and sublingual and chewable isosorbide dinitrate of 10 mg or less.
   d. Aspirin and acetaminophen in effervescent tablets or granules.
   e. Potassium supplements in unit-dose packaging.
   f. Sodium fluoride containing not more than 264 mg of sodium fluoride per package.
   g. Anhydrous cholestyramine and colestipol packets.
   h. Erythromycin ethylsuccinate granules for oral suspension and oral suspensions in packages containing no more than 8 g of erythromycin.
   i. Erythromycin ethylsuccinate tablets in packages containing no more than 16 g of erythromycin.
   j. Prednisone tablets containing no more than 105 mg per package.
   k. Methylprednisolone tablets containing no more than 84 mg per package.
   l. Mebendazole tablets containing no more than 600 mg per package.
   m. Betamethasone tablets containing no more than 12.6 mg per package.
   n. Preparations in aerosol containers intended for inhalation.
   o. Pancrelipase preparations.

p. Sucrose preparations in a solution of glycerol and water.

q. Hormone replacement therapy products that rely solely upon the activity of one or more progestogen or estrogen substances.

V. Other Federal Laws and Regulations

A. Federal Hazardous Substances Act of 1966

1. The Consumer Product Safety Commission administers and enforces this Act, which is intended to protect consumers from hazardous and toxic substances.

2. Requires the label on the immediate package of a hazardous product and any outer wrapping or container that might cover up the label on the package to have the following information in English:

   a. The name and business address of the manufacturer, packer, distributor, or seller;

   b. The common or usual or chemical name of each hazardous ingredient;

   c. The signal word "Danger" for products that are corrosive, extremely flammable, or highly toxic;

   d. The signal word "Caution" or "Warning" for all other hazardous products;

   e. An affirmative statement of the principal hazard or hazards that the product presents (e.g., "Flammable,"

"Harmful if Swallowed," "Causes Burns," "Vapor Harmful," etc.);

 f. Precautionary statements telling users what they must do or what actions they must avoid to protect themselves;

 g. Where it is appropriate, instructions for first aid treatment if the product injures someone;

 h. The word "Poison" for a product that is highly toxic, in addition to the signal word "Danger";

 i. If a product requires special care in handling or storage, instructions for consumers to follow to protect themselves; and

 j. The statement "Keep out of the reach of children." If a hazardous product such as a plant does not have a package, it still must have a hang tag that contains the required precautionary information. That information must also be printed in any literature that accompanies the product and that contains instructions for use.

 3. The act does not apply to drugs regulated by FDA, but may apply to other products sold in a pharmacy such as bleach, cleaning fluids, antifreeze, etc.

B. Hazard Communication Standard

 1. The Occupational and Safety Health Administration (OSHA) administers and enforces this regulation, which requires employers (including pharmacies) that deal with hazardous materials to meet the Hazard Communication Standard. *See 29 CFR 1910.1200.*

 2. The standard requires chemical manufacturers and importers to classify the hazards of chemicals they produce or import and to prepare appropriate labels and Safety Data Sheets (SDS), which were formerly known as Material Safety Data Sheets (MSDS).

 3. Drugs in solid, final dosage form for administration to patients are exempt from these requirements, but hazardous chemicals or products not in solid, final dosage form for administration (such as liquid products used in compounding) may be covered. Generally, a pharmacy may rely on the manufacturer to determine if a product is considered hazardous. If a pharmacy has any such products, they are required to have a written Hazard Communication Plan.

 4. The plan must include a list of hazardous chemicals in the workplace, must ensure all such products are appropriately labeled and have a Safety Data Sheet, and must include training for all workers on the hazards of chemicals, appropriate protective measures, and where and how to obtain additional information. *Note: Additional details can be found in OSHA's publication, "Small Entity Compliance Guide for Employers that Use Hazardous Chemicals."*

C. Centers for Medicare and Medicaid Services (CMS) Requirements

    1. Tamper-Resistant Prescriptions—CMS requires that all written prescriptions for covered outpatient drugs in the Medicaid program meet tamper-resistant requirements to prevent unauthorized copying and to prevent counterfeiting (with some exceptions). The tamper-evident features must include:

        a. One or more industry-recognized features designed to prevent unauthorized copying of a completed or blank prescription form;

        b. One or more industry-recognized features designed to prevent the erasure or modification of information written on the prescription pad by the prescriber; and

        c. One or more industry-recognized features designed to prevent the use of counterfeit prescription forms.

    2. Pharmacy Services at Long-Term Care Facilities:

        a. Medication Regimen Reviews—CMS regulations require a consultant pharmacist to perform a Medication Regimen Review for all long-term care patients every 30 days. The pharmacist must report any irregularities to the attending physician, the facility's medical director, and the facility's director of nursing, and these reports must be acted upon.

        b. Each resident's drug therapy must be free from unnecessary drugs. This includes drugs at excessive doses or durations and limiting psychotropic drugs to diagnosed and documented conditions.

        c. When used PRN, psychotropic drugs must be limited to 14 days unless the practitioner documents the rationale for extending an order beyond 14 days. PRN orders for psychotropic drugs cannot be renewed unless the attending physician evaluates the resident for appropriateness of that drug.

      d. To reduce medication waste, pharmacies may not dispense more than a 14-day cycle of medications to LTCF residents, with limited exceptions.

      e. Pharmacies must ensure routine and emergency drugs are provided in a timely manner to all residents. The use of emergency medication kits is permissible to help meet this requirement.

D. Delivering Prescriptions by U.S. Mail or Common Carrier

  1. Delivery by Mail (postal regulations administered by the U.S. Postal Service)—General postal regulations do not allow dangerous substances to be mailed; however, there are exceptions for prescription drugs.

      a. Non-controlled—Prescriptions containing non-controlled substances may be mailed by a pharmacy to the ultimate user provided that the medications are not alcoholic beverages, poisons, or flammable substances.

      b. Controlled substances may be mailed to patients under the following requirements:

        (1) The prescription container must be labeled in compliance with prescription labeling rules;

        (2) The outer wrapper or container in which the prescription is placed must be free of markings that would indicate the nature of the contents (including the name of the pharmacy as part of the return address on the mailing package, as that may alert individuals that drugs may be in the package); and

        (3) No markings of any kind may be placed on the package to indicate the nature of contents.

      c. Controlled substances may be mailed to other DEA registrants (practitioners, other pharmacies, distributors, or drug disposal firms) provided they are placed in a plain outer container or securely overwrapped in plain paper and all recordkeeping requirements are met.

  2. Delivery by Common Carrier—Any prescription drug may be delivered from a pharmacy to a patient by common carrier such as the United Parcel Service (UPS) or FedEx. This includes all schedules of controlled substances and dangerous drugs. Common carriers are not subject to postal regulations.

E. Federal Tax-Free Alcohol Regulations
   1. Pharmacies sometimes use 95% ethanol (190 proof) for compounding purposes.
   2. When used for scientific, medicinal, or mechanical purposes or to treat patients, such alcohol is considered "tax free."
   3. The Alcohol and Tobacco Tax and Trade Bureau (TTB) regulates tax-free alcohol with the federal Bureau of Alcohol, Tobacco, Firearms, and Explosives (ATFE). ATFE is responsible for enforcement.
   4. A user permit must be acquired from TTB and specific recordkeeping requirements must be met.
   5. Tax-free alcohol cannot be resold or used in any beverage product.

VI. Privacy—HIPAA and HITECH
   A. Most pharmacies are a "covered entity" under HIPAA and must be in compliance with these requirements.
   B. Notice and Acknowledgement
      1. Pharmacies must provide patients with a "Notice of Privacy Practices" and make a good faith effort to obtain a written acknowledgement of receipt of the Notice from the patient.
      2. The Notice must be provided upon first service delivery to the patient.
      3. The HIPAA privacy rule requires mandatory provisions in the Notice.
   C. Use and Disclosure of Protected Health Information (PHI)
      1. Protected Health Information (PHI) is the HIPAA term for patient-identifiable information.
      2. Pharmacies may use and disclose PHI to provide treatment for payment and for healthcare operations without authorization from the patient.
      3. Pharmacies may also use and disclose PHI for certain governmental functions without authorization from the patient. This includes uses and disclosures for public health activities such as reporting adverse events to FDA, to health oversight agencies such as boards of pharmacies or state drug monitoring programs, and to law enforcement agencies.
      4. Other uses and disclosures, such as for marketing purposes, require a signed authorization from the patient. If the covered entity receives remuneration (i.e., payment) for the

marketing, the authorization form must expressly inform the patient of such.

5. Face-to-face communications about alternative drugs or health products are considered part of treatment and not marketing.

6. Refill reminders for a currently prescribed drug (or one that has lapsed for not more than 90 days) are not considered marketing as long as any payment made to the pharmacy in exchange for making the communication is reasonable and related to the pharmacy's cost of making the communication.

7. Minimum Necessary Standard
   a. When using and disclosing PHI, a pharmacy must make reasonable efforts to limit PHI to the minimum necessary to accomplish the intended purpose.
   b. The minimum necessary standard does not apply to disclosures to healthcare providers for treatment purposes. These disclosures would include prescription transfers or providing prescription information to physicians.
   c. The minimum necessary standard does not apply to disclosures for which the patient has signed an authorization.
   d. The minimum necessary standard does apply to disclosures for payment.

8. Incidental Disclosures
   a. Unintended "incidental" disclosures are not a violation of the Privacy Rule as long as reasonable safeguards are in place.
   b. Examples: Sales representatives or janitorial service members accidentally see PHI during the normal course of their jobs; a customer overhears counseling that is performed in a private area in a discreet manner.
   Note: PHI must be properly disposed of by pharmacies. Pharmacies have been fined for improperly disposing of PHI (such as labeled pharmacy vials and paper records) into dumpsters accessible to the public and unauthorized individuals.

D. Business Associates (BAs)
   1. BAs are persons or entities, other than members of a pharmacy's workforce, who perform a function or service on behalf of the pharmacy that requires the use or disclosure of PHI.

2. Pharmacies are required to enter into business associate contracts with these BAs, which require the BAs to meet many of the same requirements for protecting PHI as a covered entity under HIPAA.

E. Patient Rights and Administrative Requirements
   1. Patients have a right to access and obtain a copy of their PHI. Pharmacies must comply with a request within 30 days but may extend time by no more than 30 additional days if they notify the individual of the reason for the delay.
   2. Patients have a right to amend their PHI records and request an accounting of disclosures of their PHI made by a pharmacy under certain circumstances. Pharmacies must comply with a request to amend or request for an accounting of disclosures within 60 days, but may extend it by no more than 30 additional days if they notify the individual of the reason for the delay.
   3. Pharmacies must establish policies and procedures to protect from accidental or intentional uses and disclosures of PHI through the use of appropriate administrative, technical, and physical safeguards to protect the privacy of PHI.
   4. Pharmacies must train all employees on privacy policies and impose sanctions on employees for any violations of privacy policies.
   5. Pharmacies must designate a Privacy Official who is responsible for development and implementation of HIPAA-related policies and procedures and compliance.
   6. Pharmacies must also designate a contact person to receive complaints. This person may also be the Privacy Official.

F. HITECH Act—The HITECH Act amended HIPAA to strengthen many of its provisions. Among other things, the HITECH Act added a breach notification requirement that requires:
   1. Covered entities, including pharmacies, to notify individuals of a breach of their "unsecured" PHI within 60 calendar days after the breach is discovered.
   2. BAs must report any breaches of unsecured PHI to the covered entity and provide the identities of each affected individual.
   3. A "breach" is defined as unauthorized acquisition, access, use, or disclosure of PHI that compromises its security or privacy. It does not include instances in which there has been an inadvertent disclosure from an authorized individual to

another person authorized to access PHI within the same organization. A breach also does not include instances in which the covered entity or BA has a good faith belief that the PHI is not further acquired, accessed, retained, used, or disclosed.

4. For breaches affecting fewer than 500 individuals, covered entities must maintain a log of these breaches and notify HHS of these breaches annually.

5. If more than 500 individuals are affected, the Secretary of HHS and prominent local media must be notified in addition to the affected individuals within 60 days after the breach is discovered.

CHAPTER THREE
Federal Controlled Substances Act (FCSA) and Applicable Rules

CHAPTER THREE
Federal Controlled Substances Act (FCSA) and Applicable Rules

I. Drug Classification

A. Schedule I (C-I) Drugs
1. High potential for abuse and severe potential for dependence (addiction).
2. No currently accepted medical use in treatment in the U.S.
3. Lack of accepted information on the safety of their use under medical supervision.
4. Include opiates and derivatives such as heroin and dihydromorphine; hallucinogens such as marijuana, lysergic acid diethylamide (LSD), peyote, and mescaline; and depressants such as methaqualone.

STUDY TIP: While many states have "legalized" medical or recreational use of marijuana, it is still a Schedule I controlled substance under federal law and is technically illegal. Since the stricter law applies, for purposes of the MPJE it is recommended that you treat marijuana as a Schedule I controlled substance. However, because the MPJE competencies include a reference to medical marijuana, you should be familiar with any requirements for dispensing medical marijuana that require pharmacist involvement or licensure from the Board of Pharmacy. *See also discussion in Chapter 1.*

B. Schedule II (C-II) Drugs
1. High potential for abuse.
2. Have currently accepted medical use in treatment in the U.S. or currently accepted medical use with severe restrictions.
3. Abuse of the drug or other substances may lead to severe physical or psychological dependence (addiction).
4. Include opium and other narcotics such as morphine, codeine, dihydrocodeine, oxycodone, acetaminophen with hydrocodone (Vicodin®), methadone, meperidine, hydromorphone, fentanyl, and cocaine; stimulants such as amphetamine, methamphetamine, phenmetrazine, and methylphenidate; and depressants such as

pentobarbital, secobarbital, amobarbital, glutethimide, and phencyclidine.

C. Schedule III (C-III) Drugs
1. Potential for abuse less than Schedule I or II.
2. Have currently accepted medical use in treatment in the U.S.
3. Abuse of the drug or other substance may lead to moderate or low physical dependence (addiction) or high psychological dependence (addiction).
4. Include some narcotic Schedule II drugs, but in combination with another ingredient such as aspirin with codeine or acetaminophen with codeine (e.g., Tylenol #3). Also includes some nonnarcotic drugs, including suppository forms of amobarbital, secobarbital, or pentobarbital; stimulants such as chlorphentermine, phendimetrazine, and benzphetamine; anabolic steroids including testosterone; ketamine; paregoric; and Fiorinal®, a combination of butalbital, aspirin, and caffeine.
   Note: While Fiorinal® is a Schedule III controlled substance, Fioricet®, a combination of butalbital, acetaminophen, and caffeine, is an exempt prescription drug product (see F. below) and is not labeled as a controlled substance under federal law. It may be a controlled substance under some state laws.

D. Schedule IV (C-IV) Drugs
1. Low potential for abuse relative to Schedule III.
2. Have currently accepted medical use in treatment in the U.S.
3. Abuse may lead to limited physical or psychological dependence (addiction) relative to Schedule III.
4. Include narcotics such as dextropropoxyphene and products with not more than 1 mg of difenoxin and not less than 25 mcgs of atropine sulfate per dosage unit; depressants such as alprazolam, chloral hydrate, diazepam, lorazepam, and

phenobarbital; stimulants such as diethylpropion and phentermine; and other drugs such as carisoprodol, tramadol, pentazocine, and butorphanol.

STUDY TIP: Be careful with drugs that have similar names but are in different schedules, such as phenmetrazine (C-II), phendimetrazine (C-III), and phentermine (C-IV).

E. Schedule V (C-V) Drugs
   1. Low potential for abuse relative to Schedule IV.
   2. Have currently accepted medical use in treatment in the U.S.
   3. Abuse of the drug or other substance may lead to limited physical or psychological dependence (addiction) relative to Schedule IV.
   4. Include pregabalin (Lyrica®), antitussive products containing codeine, antidiarrheal products containing opium, and certain antiseizure drugs such as brivaracetam (Brivact®) and lacosamide (Vimpat®).
   Note: Hemp derivatives, including cannabidiol (CBD), were formerly considered Schedule I controlled substances, but those containing no more than 0.3% tetrahydrocannabinol (THC) were removed from the FCSA in 2018. There is also an FDA-approved prescription cannabidiol drug derived from cannabis (not from hemp), Epidiolex®, that was originally placed in Schedule V of the FCSA. In 2020, it was removed from Schedule V and is no longer a controlled substance under federal law.

STUDY TIP: Be sure you are familiar with any differences in drug schedules from the federal law found in your state controlled substances act. Some of the more common drugs that are controlled substances in some states but are not controlled substances under federal law include chorionic gonadotropin (also known as human chorionic gonadotropin, or HCG), human growth hormone (HGH), gabapentin, pseudoephedrine, and propofol.

F. Exempted Prescription Drug Products
   1. Manufacturers may apply to DEA to exempt a product or chemical from certain provisions of the Controlled Substances Act (labeling and inventory) if the product or chemical is not likely to be abused. These products may still be considered controlled substances for certain criminal

violations even though they are not labeled as controlled substances.

2. Exempted prescription drug preparations include nonnarcotic products containing small amounts of phenobarbital, butalbital, chlordiazepoxide, or meprobamate. A common example is Fiorect® (butalbital, acetaminophen, and caffeine).

3. In April 2022, DEA issued a notice of proposed rulemaking to revoke the exempted prescription product status for all butalbital products previously granted exemptions. As of the date of publication of this book, this rule was not yet adopted. If it is adopted as proposed, almost half of the products on the exempted prescription product list would lose their exemptions and become Schedule III controlled substances, including Fioricet mentioned in C.4. above.

4. The DEA Exempt Prescription Product List can be found on DEA's website.

G. Listed Chemicals or Precursor Substances

1. Listed Chemicals are chemicals that, in addition to legitimate uses, are used in manufacturing a controlled substance.

2. In addition to specific chemicals, OTC products containing ephedrine, pseudoephedrine, or phenylpropanolamine are considered Listed Chemicals.
Note: Ephedrine and phenylpropanolamine products have been removed from the market by FDA for safety reasons.

3. These products are not controlled substances under federal law but are subject to certain sales limitations and other restrictions. *See Section IX. C. below.*

STUDY TIP: More than half the states include pseudoephedrine as a controlled substance. Be sure to know what schedule it is in your state or if it is just a listed chemical.

H. Authority to Schedule Controlled Substances

1. The U.S. Attorney General, as head of the Department of Justice (which DEA is under), may add, delete, or reschedule substances.

2. Before adding, deleting, or rescheduling substances, the DEA must obtain a scientific and medical recommendation from FDA.

II. Scheduling of Compounded Controlled Substances

A. A pharmacy may compound narcotic controlled substances pursuant to a prescription. However, DEA limits the compounding of "aqueous or oleaginous solutions or solid dosage forms" to no more than a 20% concentration. DEA considers compounding of these types of products with a narcotic ingredient greater than 20% to be manufacturing even if the pharmacist has a prescription to compound the product.

B. The narcotic substance must be compounded with one or more nonnarcotic therapeutic ingredients.

STUDY TIP: You should know the concentration limits below and be able to calculate what schedule a particular compounded product would fall in. However, first be sure that the codeine or opium is being compounded with another nonnarcotic therapeutic agent. Any straight narcotic, regardless of concentration, will always be in Schedule II. For example, if codeine or opium is only being mixed with water or simple syrup, it is still a Schedule II regardless of the concentration.

C. Concentration limits
   1. Codeine.
      a. C-V limit = 200 mg/100 ml.
      b. C-III limit = 1.8 g/100 ml and 90 mg/dosage unit.

STUDY TIP: Products such as Cheracol® and Robitussin AC® contain the maximum amount of codeine allowed for Schedule V. If you add even 1 mg of codeine to these products, they would then be in Schedule III.

---

   2. Dihydrocodeine.
      a. C-V limit = 100 mg/100 ml.
      b. C-III limit = 1.8 g/100 ml and 90 mg/dosage unit.
      Note: Anything above this limit would be Schedule II.
   3. Opium.
      a. C-V limit = 100 mg/100 ml.
      b. C-III limit = 500 mg/100 ml and 25 mg/dosage unit.
   4. Morphine.
      a. C-V limit = None (no morphine products are C-V; they are either C-II or C-III).
      b. C-III limit = 50 mg/100 ml.

STUDY TIP: A compounded narcotic prescription will never be a Schedule IV.

III. Registration
    A. General Information
        1. Every person or firm that manufactures, distributes, or dispenses any controlled substances or proposes to engage in any of these activities must register with DEA.

        2. Dispensers (pharmacies and practitioners) register every 3 years with DEA.
        3. Registration form for dispensers, including pharmacies, is DEA Form 224. Renewal form for dispensers is DEA Form 224a.
        4. Dispenser registrations start with the letters "A," "B," or "F" (or "G" for Department of Defense contractors).
        5. The second letter of the prefix will normally be the first letter of the practitioner's last name for individual practitioners or the first letter of a pharmacy's or hospital's name.
    B. Mid-Level Practitioners
        1. Practitioners, other than physicians, dentists, veterinarians, or podiatrists, who are licensed, registered, or otherwise authorized under state law to dispense (includes prescribing) controlled substances in the course of professional practice.
        2. Registration begins with the letter "M."
        3. May include advanced practice registered nurses and physician assistants if the state allows them to prescribe controlled substances. Other mid-level practitioners may include ambulance services, animal shelters, and veterinary euthanasia technicians.
        4. A list of controlled substance authorities for mid-level practitioners in each state can be found at *https://www.dea diversion.usdoj.gov/drugreg/practioners/mlp_by_state.pdf.*

    C. Activities Requiring Separate Registrations
        1. Manufacturing (C-I–C-V)
        2. Distributing (C-I–C-V)
        3. Reverse Distributing (C-I–C-V)

4. Dispensing (C-II–C-V)—Includes prescribing and adminis-
      tration by practitioners and dispensing by pharmacies
   5. Conducting research (C-I)
   6. Conducting research (C-II–C-V)
   7. Conducting narcotic treatment program (C-II–C-V)
   8. Conducting chemical analysis (C-I–C-V)
   9. Importing (C-I–C-V)
   10. Exporting (C-I–C-V)
D. Verifying a DEA Registration (number)
   1. Step 1—Add 1st, 3rd, and 5th digits.
   2. Step 2—Add 2nd, 4th, and 6th digits and multiply sum by 2.
   3. Step 3—Add the sum of steps 1 and 2, and the last digit of the
      sum should correspond to the last digit of the DEA number.
   4. Example: DEA # AB1234563.
      a. $1 + 3 + 5 = 9$.
      b. $(2 + 4 + 6) \times 2 = 24$.
      c. Total $= 33$.

STUDY TIP: You should know this DEA verification formula and be able to
confirm the validity of a DEA number.

E. A separate DEA registration is required for separate locations
   1. Each pharmacy must have a separate DEA registration.
   2. DEA will sometimes issue a campus registration that may
      include multiple buildings for large hospitals or healthcare
      facilities, but this is done on a case-by-case basis.
   3. Individual practitioners, including physicians who register at
      one location but practice at other locations in the same state,
      are not required to register at those other locations if they
      only prescribe controlled substances at those facilities. If a
      practitioner maintains a supply of controlled substances at a
      second site or if the second site is in another state, he or she
      would have to have an additional registration for that site.
F. Application for Registration
   1. DEA Form 224 is used for dispensers (practitioners and
      pharmacies).
   2. Application must be signed (or electronically signed) by the
      applicant if it is for an individual such as a physician, by a partner
      if it is for a partnership, or by an officer if it is for a corporation.
   3. An applicant can authorize another individual to sign the
      application and registration renewals by filling out a Power

of Attorney granting that individual the authority and filing that Power of Attorney with the DEA Registration Unit. *Note: This may be needed if a company (e.g., a hospital corporation or a pharmacy corporation) wishes to have a pharmacist be responsible for applying and renewing the DEA registration but the pharmacist is not an officer of the corporation. Unlike the Power of Attorney to sign DEA Form 222, this Power of Attorney must be filed with DEA. See Section IV. A.7. below.*

G. Exemptions from Registration (i.e., who does not have to register with DEA)

   1. An agent or employee of any registered manufacturer, distributor, or dispenser if acting in the usual course of business or employment.

STUDY TIP: Exempted persons would include pharmacists working in a pharmacy and nurses and other employees working in a hospital or physician's office.

---

   2. A common or contract carrier or warehouseman or an employee thereof whose possession is in the usual course of business or employment.

   3. An ultimate user (patient) who possesses such substance for a lawful purpose.

   4. Officials of the U.S. Armed Services, Public Health Service, or Bureau of Prisons acting in the course of their official duties. *Note: Military and federal practitioners are exempt from having to register with DEA, and a pharmacy outside of the federal facility may legally fill a prescription issued by such a practitioner. In practice this is difficult because many pharmacy computer systems will not allow a controlled substance to be filled without a valid prescriber's DEA number, and reporting to prescription monitoring programs may not work with a DEA number. For this reason, many federal practitioners choose to obtain a DEA registration.*

H. Practitioner's Use of Hospital DEA Number

   1. Interns, residents, staff physicians, and mid-level practitioners who are agents or employees of a hospital or other institution may administer, dispense, or prescribe controlled substances under the registration of the hospital or other institution when acting in the usual course of business or employment.

   2. The hospital must assign a specific internal code for each practitioner authorized to use the hospital's DEA number, and this must be available at all times to other registrants and law enforcement agencies. This internal code shall be a suffix to the hospital's DEA number (e.g., AP1234563-10 or AP1234563-A12).

3. Controlled substance prescriptions written by these practitioners are valid and can be filled by any pharmacy, not just the hospital pharmacy where they are employed.

I. Temporary Use of Registration Upon Sale of a Pharmacy
When selling a pharmacy, if the new owner has not yet obtained a DEA registration, DEA permits the new owner to continue the business of the pharmacy under the previous owner's registration provided the following requirements are met:

1. The new owner must expeditiously apply for an appropriate DEA registration and state licensure.

2. The previous owner grants a Power of Attorney to the new owner that provides for the following:

   a. The previous owner agrees to allow the controlled substance activities of the pharmacy to be carried out under his or her DEA registration;

   b. The previous owner agrees to allow the new owner to carry out the controlled substance activities of the pharmacy, including the ordering of controlled substances, as an agent of the previous owner;

   c. The previous owner acknowledges, as the registrant, that he or she will be held accountable for any violations of controlled substance laws which may occur; and

   d. The previous owner agrees that the controlled substance activities of the pharmacy may be carried out under his or her DEA registration and shall remain in effect for no more than 45 days after the purchase date.

STUDY TIP: This temporary-use procedure is not in a DEA rule. It was authorized many years ago in a policy letter from DEA. It is a practical policy, as it makes sense to allow the new owner time to obtain a DEA registration after a change in ownership while still allowing patients to obtain refills and get prescriptions filled. An owner cannot apply for a DEA registration until they have their state pharmacy license and state controlled substance license if applicable. The 45-day limitation was in the original guidance from DEA, but some local DEA offices may permit a longer time period if needed.

IV. Ordering and Transferring Controlled Substances

A. Ordering Schedule II Controlled Substances—DEA Form 222

    1. Required for each sale or transfer of C-II drugs (except dispensing to ultimate user).

    2. Only one item may be ordered on each numbered line.

    3. Orders for etorphine hydrochloride and diprenorphine must contain only orders for these substances.

    4. The number of lines completed must be noted on the form.

    5. Name and address of supplier from whom the controlled substances are being ordered must be entered.

    6. Must be signed (or electronically signed) by the registrant (individual, partner, or officer) or by a person authorized to execute DEA Form 222 from a Power of Attorney described in 7. below.

    7. Registrant may authorize other individuals to execute forms by creating a Power of Attorney (POA). This POA does not need to be sent to DEA but must be maintained in the pharmacy. A POA must be signed by the person granting the power, the person receiving the power (called the attorney-in-fact), and two witnesses. A sample Power of Attorney form and Notice of Revocation form are provided below and can also be found at 21 CFR 1305.05(c) as well as in the DEA's *Pharmacist Manual*.

STUDY TIP: Previous DEA rules allowed the person who signed the last application or renewal to issue a POA to allow other individuals to sign DEA Form 222. Remember, that person may have signed the renewal application based on a POA from the registrant as indicated in F.3. above. The provision that allowed the person who signed the last renewal application to sign POAs for signing DEA Form 222 was removed effective October 30, 2019. This means that only the actual registrant (individual, partner, or corporate officer) may grant a POA for signing DEA Form 222.

Note: In September 2019, DEA modified the POA rule to make it clear that only the registrant (individual, partner, or corporate officer) can issue a POA to allow others to sign DEA Form 222. Despite this, the sample POA and Revocation of POA forms below that are reprinted from DEA's rule indicate it can be issued by a person authorized to sign the current application for registration. This is inconsistent with the revised POA rule, which says the only person who can issue and sign a POA is the actual registrant (individual, partner, or corporate officer). If someone other than the registrant has been given authority to sign the registration applications and renewals as allowed in F.3. above, that individual cannot issue a POA authorizing others to order Schedule II controlled substances.

Sample Power of Attorney for
DEA Forms 222 and Electronic Orders

(Name of registrant)

(Address of registrant)

(DEA registration number)

I, _____ (name of person granting power), the undersigned, who is authorized to sign the current application for registration of the above-named registrant under the Controlled Substances Act or Controlled Substances Import and Export Act, have made, constituted, and appointed, and by these presents, do make, constitute, and appoint _____ (name of attorney-in-fact), my true and lawful attorney for me in my name, place, and stead, to execute applications for books of official order forms and to sign such order forms in requisition for Schedule I and II controlled substances, in accordance with Section 308 of the Controlled Substances Act (21 U.S.C. 828) and Part 1305 of Title 21 of the Code of Federal Regulations. I hereby ratify and confirm all that said attorney shall lawfully do or cause to be done by virtue hereof.

_____

(Signature of person granting power)

I, _____ (name of attorney-in-fact), hereby affirm that I am the person named herein as attorney-in-fact and that the signature affixed hereto is my signature.

_____

(Signature of attorney-in-fact)

Witnesses:

1. _____

2. _____

Signed and dated on the _____ day of _____ in the year _____ at _____.

Sample Notice of Revocation

The foregoing power of attorney is hereby revoked by the under-signed, who is authorized to sign the current application for registration of the above-named registrant under the Controlled Substances Act. Written notice of this revocation has been given to the attorney-in-fact _____
this same day.

_____

(Signature of person revoking power)

Witnesses:

1. _____

2. _____

Signed and dated on the _____ day of _____ in the year _____ at _____.

8. Forms that are not complete, legible, properly prepared, or signed will not be accepted.
9. Forms that show any alteration, erasure, or changes will not be accepted.
10. A supplier may provide a partial quantity for the requested amount, but the remaining quantity must be sent within 60 days or the order becomes void. With the exception of certain Department of Defense orders, no DEA Form 222 is valid more than 60 days after its execution by the purchaser.
11. If a completed order form is lost or stolen, purchaser must prepare another DEA Form 222, along with a statement containing the serial number and date of the lost form and stating that the goods covered by the first order were not received because the form was lost.
12. A pharmacy may fax a completed DEA Form 222 to a supplier for the supplier to prepare the order; however, the supplier may not ship the product until the original DEA Form 222 is received and verified.
13. Single Copy DEA Form 222
    a. Effective October 30, 2019, DEA finalized rules to transition from a triplicate (3-copy) DEA Form 222 to a single

copy DEA Form 222 with additional security features. There was a 2-year transition period during which existing triplicate DEA Forms 222 could be used, but as of October 30, 2021, only the single copy DEA Form 222 may be used.

    b. The single forms contain 20 order lines per form rather than 10 order lines on the triplicate forms.

    c. The purchaser filling out a single copy DEA Form 222 must make a copy of the original form for its records and submit the original form to the supplier. The copy may be retained in paper or electronic form.
Note: If kept electronically, the copy of DEA Form 222 does not need to be stored on a different server or system from the purchaser's other records. Also, electronic copies of DEA Form 222 may also be stored on a system at a location different from the registered location. However, at all times, the forms need to be readily retrievable at the registered location.

    d. The supplier may only fill an order from the original form and not from a copy. The supplier must record, on the original form, the number of containers furnished for each ordered item and the date the products are shipped to the purchaser.
Note: There was some confusion as to whether the purchaser or the supplier had to fill out the DEA number of the supplier on the single copy form because the instructions for that part of the form state that it is to be entered by the purchaser. This was different from the previous triplicate DEA Form 222, which required the supplier to fill out that section. DEA clarified that the purchaser should enter that information, but if it is omitted, the supplier may complete that part of the form. See 86 Fed. Reg. 38230 (July 20, 2021).

    e. Most suppliers (e.g., wholesalers) are required to report the acquisition and disposition of Schedule II and certain Schedule III and IV controlled substances to DEA's Automation of Reports and Consolidated Orders System (ARCOS). A supplier who reports transactions to ARCOS is not required to send a copy of the original DEA Form 222 to DEA because this information is already reported to ARCOS. However, if a supplier is not required to report transactions to ARCOS (e.g., a pharmacy or practitioner acting as a supplier under the 5% rule), they must submit a copy of the original DEA Form 222 to DEA either by mail or by email to *DEA.Orderforms@usdoj.gov* when acting as a supplier. *Note: When a pharmacy acts as a supplier, in addition to submitting a copy of DEA Form 222 to DEA by mail or email, the pharmacy must have a system to identify any suspicious orders, which when identified must be reported online to DEA's Suspicious Orders Report System (SORS).*

f. When the product has been received, the purchaser must record the number of containers received and the date received for each item on the copy of the DEA Form 222 they made when ordering the product.

STUDY TIP: The person receiving the controlled substances (purchaser) always provides the original DEA Form 222 to the supplier and makes a copy for their records to record the products received.

---

14. Electronic Ordering of Schedule II Controlled Substances

    a. DEA allows electronic ordering of Schedule II controlled substances through the Controlled Substances Ordering System (CSOS).

    b. Each pharmacy must appoint a CSOS coordinator who will serve as that pharmacy's recognized agent regarding issues pertaining to issuance of, revocation of, and changes to digital certificates issued under that registrant's DEA registration.

    c. It allows electronic orders based on digital certificates issued by the DEA Certification Authority that are valid until the expiration of the DEA registration for the facility (3 years).

    d. Even though each CSOS Certificate expires when the DEA registration of the facility expires, they are issued to *individual subscribers*. Certificates must never be used by anyone other than the individual subscriber (a person, not a location) the certificate was issued to.

    e. There are two types of CSOS Certificates:

        (1) CSOS Administrative Certificates are used to digitally sign communications with DEA as well as with other participants in the CSOS community. Administrative Certificates are issued only to CSOS Coordinators and are not valid for electronic ordering.

        (2) CSOS Signing Certificates are used for digitally signing controlled substance orders. Signing certificates are issued to approved Registrant and Power of Attorney applicants. Approved Coordinator applicants will only be issued a Signing certificate if he/she holds valid Power of Attorney for controlled substance ordering and has requested a Signing certificate on his/her CSOS Certificate Application.

    f. All CSOS applications must be audited by an independent third-party auditor prior to use and whenever changes are made to the software to ensure that the software is in compliance with DEA regulations.

    g. An electronic order for controlled substances may not be filled if any of the following occurs:

        (1) The required data fields have not been completed.

        (2) The order is not signed using a digital certificate issued by DEA.

        (3) The digital certificate used has expired or been revoked prior to signature.

        (4) The purchaser's public key will not validate the digital certificate.

        (5) The validation of the order shows that the order is invalid for any reason.

    h. If an order cannot be filled, the supplier must notify the purchaser and provide a statement as to the reason (e.g., improperly prepared or altered). A supplier may, for any reason, refuse to accept any order. If a supplier refuses, a statement that the order is not accepted is sufficient.

    i. When a purchaser receives an unaccepted electronic order from the supplier, the purchaser must electronically link the statement of nonacceptance to the original order. The original statement must be retained for two years. Neither a purchaser nor a supplier may correct a defective order. The purchaser must issue a new order for the order to be filled.

Note: For details on CSOS, see DEA's eCommerce website at https://www.deaecom.gov/csosmain.html.

B. Ordering Schedule III–V Controlled Substances

1. Schedule III–V controlled substances can be ordered through normal ordering processes from a wholesaler or manufacturer, but pharmacies must retain documentation of the receipt of the products in the form of an invoice provided by the wholesaler or manufacturer.

2. The invoice must contain:

    a. Name of controlled substance.

    b. Dosage form and strength.

    c. Number of units per container (e.g., 100-tablet bottle).

    d. Quantity received (containers).

    e. Date of receipt.

    f. Name, address, and DEA number of the registrant from where the controlled substance was received.

STUDY TIP: It is recommended that you memorize the required elements on an invoice for Schedule III–V controlled substances.

C. Transfers of Controlled Substances Between Registrants— The 5% Rule

1. A pharmacy does not have to register with DEA as a distributor as long as total quantities of controlled substances distributed during a 12-month period in which the pharmacy is registered do not exceed 5% of the total quantity of all controlled substances dispensed and distributed during that same 12-month period.

2. Example: A pharmacy dispenses and distributes a total of 100,000 doses (e.g., tablets, capsules, teaspoons, etc.) of all controlled substances (not just Schedule II drugs). This pharmacy would be allowed to transfer 5,000 doses without being registered with DEA as a distributor.

3. If the transfer is for a Schedule II controlled substance, a DEA Form 222 is required. For Schedule III–V controlled substances, an invoice provided by the supplier (i.e., the pharmacy) is required with the required elements as listed in B.2. above.

4. Transfers can only be made to the address listed on a DEA registration. This applies to all controlled substances, not just Schedule II controlled substances.

STUDY TIP: Notice that for Schedule II controlled substances, the person receiving the product initiates and fills out the DEA Form 222, which is sent to the supplier or seller. However, for Schedule III–V controlled substances, the invoice is provided by the supplier or seller to the purchaser.

V. Destruction of Controlled Substances

A. Disposal and Destruction of Stock Controlled Substances (21 CFR 1317.01–1317. 95)

    1. On-site destruction of controlled substances in a pharmacy must be done using DEA Form 41, which requires the name and NDC number of the drug, and the strength, dosage form, package size, and quantity of the controlled substances destroyed. It also requires recording the method by which the drugs were destroyed and two signatures of employees who witnessed the destruction. A sample DEA Form 41 is provided on the next page.
Note: DEA Form 41 is also used to document destruction of controlled substances that a pharmacy received as an authorized collector even though these drugs are not "stock" controlled substances because they are not part of the pharmacy's inventory. See Section B. below.

    2. Destruction of controlled substances must be done in compliance with all state and federal laws, and the method of destruction shall be sufficient to render all such controlled substances non-retrievable.

    3. Non-retrievable is defined as "to permanently alter any controlled substance's physical and/or chemical condition or state through irreversible means in order to render the controlled substance unavailable and unusable for all practical purposes."
Note: This can be difficult to execute. In addition to the difficulty of complying with other laws such as EPA laws, DEA has stated that methods such as mixing controlled substances with items such as kitty litter or coffee grounds and depositing in the garbage do not meet the non-retrievable standard. For these reasons, most pharmacies do not participate in on-site destruction.

4. Because it is difficult to comply with all other laws including environmental requirements, most community pharmacies do not use this method of destruction, but it may be utilized in other practice settings such as hospitals.
5. Transfer to an Authorized (Registered) Reverse Distributor
   a. This is the preferred method of destruction of controlled substance inventory in a pharmacy and is simply a transfer from one DEA registrant (the pharmacy) to another (the reverse distributor).
   b. Because this is a transfer, a DEA Form 41 is not required. The transfer must be documented with an invoice for Schedule III–V controlled substances and a DEA Form 222 for Schedule II controlled substances.

STUDY TIP: Be sure to understand the difference between use of a DEA Form 41, which is used to destroy controlled substances on the premises of a pharmacy (even though this is not often done in community practice), and transferring controlled substances to a DEA-registered reverse distributor for destruction, which requires a DEA Form 222 or an invoice.

B. Destruction of Dispensed Controlled Substances—Authorized Collectors and DEA Take-Back Events
   1. DEA rules allow pharmacies to modify their DEA registrations to serve as a collector of controlled substances from ultimate users, including patients, the personal representative of the patient in the event of the patient's death, and at long-term care facilities (i.e., dispensed controlled substances).
   2. A pharmacy or hospital is not required to serve as a collector.
   3. The following rules apply to Authorized Collectors:
      a. Collectors may allow ultimate users (patients) to deposit controlled substances into collection receptacles at the registered location (or at an authorized LTCF).
      b. The controlled substances may be commingled with non-controlled substances.
      c. The deposited substances may not be counted, sorted, inventoried, or individually handled. This means that the pharmacist should not be handling these controlled substances on the patient's behalf. Patients must be the ones who place the controlled substances into the collection receptacles.

U. S. DEPARTMENT OF JUSTICE – DRUG ENFORCEMENT ADMINISTRATION
REGISTRANT RECORD OF CONTROLLED SUBSTANCES DESTROYED
FORM DEA-41

A. REGISTRANT INFORMATION

Registered Name:		DEA Registration Number:
Registered Address:		
City:	State:	Zip Code:
Telephone Number:		Contact Name:

B. ITEM DESTROYED
1. Inventory

	National Drug Code or DEA Controlled Substances Code Number	Batch Number	Name of Substance	Strength	Form	Pkg. Qty.	Number of Full Pkgs.	Partial Pkg. Count	Total Destroyed
Examples	16590-598-60	N/A	Kadian	60mg	Capsules	60	2	0	120 Capsules
	0555-0767-02	N/A	Adderall	5mg	Tablet	100	0	83	83 Tablets
	9050	B02120312	Codeine	N/A	Bulk	1.25 kg	N/A	N/A	1.25 kg
1.									
2.									
3.									
4.									
5.									
6.									
7.									

2. Collected Substances

	Returned Mail-Back Package	Sealed Inner Liner	Unique Identification Number	Size of Sealed Inner Liner	Quantity of Package(s)/Liner(s) Destroyed
Examples	X		MBP1106, MBP1108 - MBP1110, MBP112	N/A	5
		X	CRL1007 - CRL1027	15 gallon	21
		X	CRL1201	5 gallon	1
1.					
2.					
3.					
4.					
5.					
6.					
7.					

Form DEA-41   *See instructions on reverse (page 2) of form.*

C. METHOD OF DESTRUCTION

Date of Destruction:	Method of Destruction:	
Location or Business Name:		
Address:		
City:	State:	Zip Code:

D. WITNESSES

I declare under penalty of perjury, pursuant to 18 U.S.C. 1001, that I personally witnessed the destruction of the above-described controlled substances to a non-retrievable state and that all of the above is true and correct.

Printed name of first authorized employee witness:	Signature of first witness:	Date:
Printed name of second authorized employee witness:	Signature of second witness:	Date:

E. INSTRUCTIONS

1. Section A. REGISTRANT INFORMATION: The registrant destroying the controlled substance(s) shall provide their DEA registration number and the name and address indicated on their valid DEA registration, in addition to a current telephone number and a contact name, if different from the name on the valid DEA registration.

2. Section B. (1) Inventory: This part shall be used by registrants destroying lawfully possessed controlled substances, other than those described in Section B(2). In each row, indicate the National Drug Code (NDC) for the controlled substance destroyed, or if the substance has no NDC, indicate the DEA Controlled Substances Code Number for the substance; if the substance destroyed is in bulk form, indicate the batch number, if available. In each row, indicate the name, strength, and form of the controlled substance destroyed, and the number of capsules, tablets, etc., that are in a full package (pkg. qty.). If destroying the full quantity of the controlled substance, indicate the number of packages destroyed (number of full pkgs.). If destroying a partial package, indicate the partial count of the capsules, tablets, etc. destroyed (partial pkg. count). If destroying a controlled substance in bulk form, indicate that the substance is in bulk form (form) and the weight of the substance destroyed (pkg. qty.). In each row, indicate the total number of each controlled substance destroyed (total destroyed).

3. Section B. (2) Collected Substances: This part shall be used by registrants destroying controlled substances obtained through an authorized collection activity in accordance with 21 U.S.C. 822(g). In each row, indicate whether registrant is destroying a mail-back package or an inner liner. If destroying a mail-back package, enter each unique identification number separated by a comma and/or as a list in a sequential range and total quantity of packages being destroyed. If destroying an inner liner, enter each unique identification number separated by a comma and/or as a list in a sequential range based on the size of the liners destroyed and the total quantity of inner liners being destroyed. In the case of mail-back packages or inner liners received from a law enforcement agency which do not have a unique identification number or clearly marked size, include the name of the law enforcement agency and, if known, the size of the inner liner or package. DO NOT OPEN ANY MAIL-BACK PACKAGE OR INNER LINER; AN INVENTORY OF THE CONTENTS OF THE PACKAGES OR LINERS IS PROHIBITED BY LAW AND IS NOT REQUIRED BY THIS FORM.

4. If additional space is needed for items destroyed in Section B, attach to this form additional page(s) containing the requested information for each controlled substance destroyed.

5. Section C. METHOD OF DESTRUCTION: Provide the date, location, and method of destruction. The method of destruction must render the controlled substance to a state of non-retrievable and meet all applicable destruction requirements.

6. Section D. WITNESSES: Two authorized employees must declare by signature, under penalty of perjury, that such employees personally witnessed the destruction of the controlled substances listed in Section B in the manner described in Section C.

7. You are not required to submit this form to DEA, unless requested to do so. This form must be kept as a record of destruction and be available by the registrant for at least two years in accordance with 21 U.S.C. 827.

Paperwork Reduction Act Statement: The information collected on this form is necessary for DEA registrants to record controlled substances destroyed in accordance with the Controlled Substances Act (CSA). The records that DEA registrants maintain in accordance with the CSA must be kept and be available, for at least two years, for inspection and copying by officers or employees of the United States authorized by the Attorney General. 21 U.S.C. 827. DEA estimates that it will take approximately 30 minutes to complete this form, including the time for reviewing instructions, searching existing data sources, gathering and maintaining the data needed, and completing and reviewing the collection of information. The completion of this form by DEA registrants that destroy controlled substances is mandatory in accordance with 21 U.S.C. 827. Please note that an agency may not conduct or sponsor, and a person is not required to respond to, a collection of information unless it displays a currently valid OMB control number. Comments regarding this information collection, including suggestions for reducing the burden estimate, should be directed to the Drug Enforcement Administration, DEA Federal Register Representative/ODL, 8701 Morrissette Drive, Springfield, Virginia 22152.

d. LTCF staff may dispose of a patient's controlled substances into an authorized collection receptacle. Disposal into a collection receptacle must occur within three business days after the discontinuation of use by the patient.

e. Collection receptacles must be in the immediate proximity (where they can be seen) of where controlled substances are stored (i.e., the pharmacy).

f. Collection receptacles must be securely fastened to a permanent structure, locked, and securely constructed with a permanent outer container and a removable inner container.

g. The inner liner must be waterproof, tamper-evident, removable, and able to be sealed immediately upon removal with no emptying or touching the contents or ability to view the contents. The inner liner also must have a permanent unique identification number that allows tracking.

h. The inner liner must be removed by or under the supervision of at least two employees of the Authorized Collector.

i. Sealed inner liners may not be opened, x-rayed, analyzed, or otherwise penetrated.

j. Collectors can either destroy the collected drugs on-site, transfer the collected drugs for final disposal to a DEA-registered reverse distributor, or contact the DEA Special Agent in Charge for assistance. If destroyed on-site, DEA Form 41 would be utilized. Section 2 of DEA Form 41 is for "collected substances." Instead of indicating the specific controlled substances being destroyed, it requires the unique identification number of the inner liner from the collection receptacle or the mail-back package.

4. A pharmacy that serves as a collector may also operate a mail-back program for collection of dispensed controlled substances. Packages used in a mail-back program must:

a. Be nondescript and shall not have any markings or other information that might indicate that the package contains controlled substances;

b. Be waterproof, tamper-evident, tear-resistant, and sealable;

    c. Be pre-addressed with and delivered to the collector's registered address;

    d. Include prepaid shipping costs;

    e. Have a unique identification number to enable tracking; and

    f. Include instructions for the user.

STUDY TIP: A collector that conducts a mail-back program may only accept packages that the collector made available. If the collector receives a package that the collector did not make available, the collector must notify DEA within three business days of receipt.

---

    5. DEA also conducts Drug Take Back Days to collect controlled substances (and other drugs) from ultimate users.

    6. Disposal of Controlled Substances of a Hospice Patient by Employees of the Hospice.

       a. The SUPPORT Act, a comprehensive opioid bill passed by Congress in late 2018, authorizes an employee of a qualified hospice program to handle controlled substances, which were lawfully dispensed to a person receiving hospice care, for the purpose of destruction.

       b. DEA has yet to adopt regulations to implement this law and practice.

C. Waste of Controlled Substances

    1. Waste of a controlled substance occurs when a controlled substance has been removed from inventory in accordance with a physician's order for administration to a patient and is not entirely administered to the patient.

    2. Wasting of a partial quantity of a controlled substance does not require use of a DEA Form 41. The controlled substance has already been accounted for since it was ordered for and administered to a patient. Any remaining quantity from a syringe or bottle that needs to be wasted can be done following any state laws or rules or hospital policy.

    3. Many states require such waste to be witnessed (usually with two witnesses) and documentation that includes the date, quantity wasted, and method of disposal.

STUDY TIP: Do not get the destruction of controlled substances rules mixed up with wasting of controlled substances.

VI. Additional Requirements for Controlled Substances
A. Storage and Security
1. Pharmacies may store controlled substances in a secure cabinet that is locked.
2. Pharmacies may store controlled substances by dispersal throughout the non-controlled stock to deter theft.
3. Pharmacies may not store all controlled substances on one unsecured shelf.

STUDY TIP: While many pharmacies keep some or all their controlled substances in locked storage, it is not a legal requirement under federal law. Some states have stricter requirements for security, so be sure to check the requirements under your state law.

B. Theft or Significant Loss
1. A theft or significant loss of controlled substances must be reported in writing to DEA within one business day of discovery of the theft or significant loss. DEA also recommends notifying local police.

STUDY TIP: Any theft must be reported, but only "significant" losses. Check your state requirements for reporting also. Many state controlled substance agencies and/or boards of pharmacy have similar reporting requirements. There may also be required reporting to state or local law enforcement agencies.

2. Complete DEA Form 106 (Theft or Loss of Controlled Substances). This form can be filled out online at DEA's website.
3. Submitting DEA Form 106 immediately is not necessary if the pharmacy needs time to investigate the facts, but an initial notification must be provided in writing to DEA within one business day of discovery. Although not in the rule, DEA advises that if the investigation lasts longer than 60 days, the pharmacy needs to provide an update to DEA.
Note: At the time of publication of this book, DEA had proposed revising this rule to require that the DEA Form 106 be filed within 15 days of discovery. It also would require the form to be filled out online, which almost everyone already does. You should check to see if this rule was adopted as proposed or modified, although it is unlikely to be on the MPJE if it was only recently adopted.

4. The DEA *Pharmacist Manual* provides the following guidance on determining whether a loss is significant and needs to be reported.

    a. Whether a "significant loss" has occurred depends, in large part, on the business of the pharmacy and the likelihood of a rational explanation for a particular occurrence. What would constitute a significant loss for a pharmacy may be viewed as comparatively insignificant for a hospital or manufacturer.

    b. The loss of a small quantity of controlled substances, repeated over a period of time, may indicate a significant problem for a registrant, which must be reported.

    c. When determining whether a loss is significant, a registrant should consider, among others, the following factors:

        (1) The actual quantity of controlled substances lost in relation to the type of business;

        (2) The specific controlled substances;

        (3) Whether the loss of the controlled substances can be associated with access to those controlled substances by specific individuals, or whether the loss can be attributed to unique activities that may take place involving the controlled substances;

        (4) A pattern of losses over a specific time period, whether the losses appear to be random, and the results of efforts taken to resolve the losses;

        (5) Whether the specific controlled substances are likely candidates for diversion; and

        (6) Local trends and other indicators of the diversion potential of the missing controlled substances.

5. Reporting Losses of Listed Chemicals (primarily pseudoephedrine products in a pharmacy)

    a. DEA requires any unusual or excessive loss or disappearance (this would include a theft) of a listed chemical to be reported to DEA at the earliest practicable opportunity.

    b. A written report must be provided within 15 days and must include a description of the circumstances of the loss (in-transit, theft from premises, etc.).

C. Miscellaneous DEA Rules and Policies

    1. Convicted Felon Rule—A pharmacy cannot employ someone who has access to controlled substances if the person has been convicted of a felony involving controlled substances unless a waiver is granted by DEA.

2. Employee Screening Procedures—DEA requires pharmacies to screen potential employees with specific questions regarding criminal history and use of controlled substances.

3. Employee Responsibility to Report Drug Diversion—Individual employees are required to report any diversion by other employees to a responsible security official of the employer.

4. Hospital Patient's Possession of Controlled Substances—

   a. When a patient is admitted to a hospital via ambulance and no family is present with them, and if the patient has in their possession a legal controlled substance that is medically appropriate for the patient to continue taking, the hospital could secure the medication with the patient's belongings in the patient's hospital room (e.g., in a secured lockbox). Following this guidance avoids the hospital from taking unlawful possession of the controlled substance.

   b. When the patient is admitted with no family present and it has been determined inappropriate for the patient to continue taking the medication(s), or if the hospital has a policy against it, then the hospital has the following options:

      (1) If a family member arrives at the hospital, the medications can be turned over to him or her to take the medications back to the house and/or dispose of them. Or, if the hospital has mail-back packages, these can be provided for the family member, and then sealed to mail to a DEA-registered reverse distributor for disposal. Lastly, if the hospital is an authorized collector, the family member can dispose of the medications in the hospital's collection receptacle.

      (2) If no family member arrives, the medications are considered abandoned, and the hospital should contact local law enforcement or the local DEA office for guidance. Alternatively, if the state has a law addressing this matter, that law can be followed.

5. Federal Transfer Warning (21 CFR 209.5)—The following warning is required to be on the label of Schedule II–IV controlled substances when dispensed to a patient: "Caution: Federal law prohibits the transfer of this drug to any person

other than the patient for whom it was prescribed." The only exception would be for a controlled substance dispensed in a "blinded" clinical study.

6. DEA Guidelines for Emergency Kits in Long Term Care Facilities
   a. A pharmacy may place an emergency kit with controlled substances in a non-DEA-registered Long Term Care Facility (LTCF) if the appropriate state agency or regulatory authority specifically approves the placement.
   b. State law must have procedures that specify:
      (1) The source from which the LTCF may obtain controlled substances for emergency kits and that the source of supply is a DEA-registered hospital/clinic, pharmacy, or practitioner.
      (2) The security safeguards for each emergency kit stored at the LTCF, including who may have access to the emergency kit, and specific limitation of the type and quantity of controlled substances permitted in the kit.
      (3) The responsibility for proper control and accountability of the emergency kit within the LTCF, including the requirement that the LTCF and the supplying registrant maintain complete and accurate records of the controlled substances placed in the emergency kit, the disposition of the controlled substances, and the requirement to take and maintain periodic physical inventories.
      (4) The emergency medical conditions under which the controlled substances may be administered to LTCF patients, including the requirement that controlled substances be administered by authorized personnel only as expressly authorized by an individual practitioner and in compliance with DEA rules.

D. Inventories
   1. An initial inventory is required on the first day a pharmacy is open for business. If no controlled substances are in stock, a zero inventory should be recorded.
   2. Federal law requires a controlled substance inventory biennially (every two years), and that inventory must be maintained in the pharmacy. The inventory may be done on the pharmacy's regular physical inventory date, which is nearest to, and does not vary by more than six months from, the biennial date that would apply.

   3. Newly scheduled drugs or drugs moved from one schedule to another must be inventoried on the day scheduled or moved to a new schedule.
   4. Inventory records must contain:
      a. The date of the inventory;
      b. Whether the inventory was taken at the beginning or close of business;
      c. The name of each controlled substance inventoried;
      d. The finished form of each of the substances (e.g., 10 mg tablet);
      e. The number of dosage units of each finished form in the commercial container (e.g., 100-tablet bottle);
      f. The number of commercial containers of each finished form (e.g., four 100-tablet bottles); and
      g. A count of the substance.
   5. Inventory Counts.
      a. An exact count is required for all Schedule IIs.
      b. An estimated count is allowed for Schedule III–V products unless the container holds more than 1,000 tablets or capsules.

E. Records
   1. Records of controlled substances must be maintained for two years under the FCSA.
   2. DEA requires that records and inventories of Schedule II controlled substances be kept separately from all other records. Records and inventories of Schedule III–V controlled substances must be maintained separately or be "readily retrievable" from other records. "Readily retrievable" means the record is kept or maintained in such a manner that it can be separated out from all other records in a reasonable time or that it is identified by an asterisk, a redline, or some other identifiable manner such that it is easily distinguishable from all other records.
   3. Records of Receipt of Controlled Substances.
      a. C-II—Copy 3 of DEA Form 222 or copy of original single page DEA Form 222 (with the number of containers and date received filled in).
      b. C-III–C-V—Supplier's invoice.
   4. Records of Disbursement of Controlled Substances.
      a. Most pharmacies maintain records of dispensing in an electronic system (i.e., computer system). DEA has specific requirements for electronic records of prescriptions as follows:
         (1) The electronic system must provide online retrieval of original prescription information and current refill history for those prescriptions which are currently authorized for refill.
         (2) The pharmacist must verify and document that the refill data entered into the system is correct.
         (3) The system must be able to produce a hard-copy printout of each day's controlled substance prescription refills, and each pharmacist who refilled those prescriptions must verify his/her accuracy by signing and dating the printout as he/she would sign a check or legal document. This daily printout must

be printed within 72 hours of the date refills were dispensed.

Note: Most pharmacies do not print out this daily hard copy and instead use the alternative procedure in (4) below.

(4) Instead of the daily printout, a pharmacy can maintain a bound logbook or a separate file in which each pharmacist involved in the day's dispensing signs a statement verifying that the refill information entered into the computer that day has been reviewed by him/her and is correct as shown.

(5) A pharmacy's electronic system must have the capability of printing out any refill data, which the pharmacy must maintain under the CSA. For example, this would include a refill-by-refill audit trail for any specified strength and dosage form of any controlled substance, by either brand or generic name or both, dispensed by the pharmacy. Such a printout must include:

(i) Prescribing practitioner's name;

(ii) Patient's name and address;

(iii) Quantity and date dispensed on each refill;

(iv) Name or identification code of the dispensing pharmacist; and

(v) Original prescription number.

STUDY TIP: These are antiquated rules, but you need to know them. These rules were put in place when pharmacies were transitioning from a manual recordkeeping system to an electronic recordkeeping system. In a manual recordkeeping system, DEA rules still require the pharmacist to document all refills of controlled substances on the back of the hard copy of the prescription by indicating the date refilled and pharmacist's initials.

---

b. Prescription Files—Although most pharmacies maintain electronic dispensing records, there are still specific storage requirements for the hard copies of written controlled substance prescriptions or verbal prescriptions reduced to writing. Storage options:

(1) 3-file storage system:

File #1 = Schedule II only.

File #2 = Schedule III–V.

File #3 = Non-controlled drugs.

(2) 2-file storage system:

Note: Not many pharmacies use this, but it is still in the DEA rules.

File #1—Schedule II only.

File #2—Schedule III–V and non-controlled drugs. With this system, controlled substance prescriptions have to be stamped with red ink in the lower right corner of the prescription with a "C" (not less than 1 inch in height) so as to be readily retrievable from non-controlled substances.

Note: If a pharmacy maintains records in a data processing system for prescriptions (i.e., a computer), which permits identification by prescription number and retrieval of original documents by prescriber's name, patient's name, drug dispensed, and date filled, then the requirement to mark the hard-copy prescription with a red "C" is waived.

STUDY TIP: The file storage system requirements only apply to written prescriptions and verbal prescriptions that are reduced to writing by a pharmacist. If a controlled substance prescription is transmitted electronically, DEA requires that those electronic prescriptions be maintained electronically.

---

   c. Other records of disbursement (i.e., controlled substances that leave a pharmacy) include DEA Form 106 (Theft or Significant Loss), DEA Form 41 (Destruction), DEA Form 222 for any Schedule II distributions made under the 5% rule, and invoices for Schedule III–V distributions made under the 5% rule.

F. Central Recordkeeping

  1. A pharmacy wishing to maintain shipping and financial records at a central location other than the registered location must notify the nearest DEA Diversion Field Office.

  2. Unless the pharmacy is notified by DEA that permission to keep the central records is denied, the pharmacy may begin maintaining central records 14 days after notifying DEA.

  3. Central records shall not include executed DEA order forms (the copy of DEA Form 222 made by the pharmacy with number of containers and date received entered), prescriptions (actual physical prescriptions or electronic prescriptions), or inventories. These must be kept at the pharmacy.

VII. Dispensing Controlled Substance Prescriptions

A. Corresponding Responsibility

    1. For a prescription for a controlled substance to be valid, it must be issued for a legitimate medical purpose by an individual practitioner acting in the usual scope of his or her professional practice.

    2. The responsibility for the proper prescribing and dispensing of a controlled substance is upon the prescribing practitioner, but a corresponding responsibility rests with the pharmacist who fills the prescription. This means a pharmacist cannot simply rely on the fact that a physician has a valid DEA registration to determine if a controlled substance prescription is valid.

    3. Through enforcement actions, DEA has identified a number of "red flags" that may require a pharmacist to do further investigation as to the legitimacy of controlled substance prescriptions. There are several lists of "red flags" available from various sources, and some states may have specific rules addressing this topic. Typical "red flags" include:

        a. Substantially identical prescriptions for the same controlled substances, potentially paired with other drugs, for numerous persons indicating a lack of individual drug therapy in prescriptions issued by the practitioner;

        b. Prescriptions by a prescriber that are routinely for controlled substances commonly known to be abused drugs, including opioids, benzodiazepines, muscle relaxants, psychostimulants, and/or cough syrups containing codeine, or any combination of these drugs;

        c. Prescriptions for controlled substances by a prescriber that contain nonspecific or no diagnoses or lack the intended use of the drug;

        d. Prescriptions for controlled substances for the highest strength of the drug and/or for large quantities (e.g., monthly supply), indicating a lack of individual drug therapy in prescriptions issued by the practitioner;

        e. The controlled substance(s) or the quantity of the controlled substance(s) prescribed is/are inconsistent with the practitioner's area of medical practice;

    f. The Prescription Monitoring Program indicates the person presenting the prescriptions is obtaining similar drugs from multiple practitioners and/or that the person is being dispensed similar drugs at multiple pharmacies;

    g. Multiple persons with the same address present substantially similar controlled substance prescriptions from the same practitioner;

    h. Persons consistently pay for controlled substance prescriptions with cash or cash equivalents more often than through insurance; and

    i. Persons presenting controlled substance prescriptions are doing so in such a manner that varies from the manner in which persons routinely seek pharmacy services (e.g., persons arriving in the same vehicle with prescriptions from the same practitioner; one person seeking to pick up prescriptions for multiple others; and drugs referenced by street names).

B. Written Controlled Substance Prescriptions

  1. Must be manually signed by the practitioner and dated on the date issued.

  2. Must contain:

    a. The full name and address of the patient.

    b. The drug name, strength, and dosage form.

    c. The quantity prescribed.
    Note: Some states require that the quantity prescribed must be written numerically and textually (as a word). Example: Vicodin #20 (twenty).

    d. Directions for use.

    e. Number of refills authorized, if any (not for Schedule II).

    f. The name, address, and DEA number of the practitioner.

    g. If written for a Schedule II prescription to be filled at a later date, the earliest date on which a pharmacy may fill a prescription.
    Note: DEA rules also specify that a prescription for gamma-hydroxybutyric acid (GHB) must include the medical need of the patient for the prescription.

  3. DEA does not allow pharmacists to prepopulate a controlled substance prescription with all required information and then fax or electronically send the prescription to a practitioner to be signed.

Note: This is interesting because DEA does not take issue with pharmacists calling to get refill authorization for a controlled substance prescription that has expired, but for a written prescription they take the position that a pharmacist is not an agent of the prescriber and therefore cannot prepare a prescription for a prescriber to sign.

C. Verbal and Fax Prescriptions
   1. Verbal prescriptions are not valid for Schedule II controlled substances unless it is an emergency.
   2. Verbal prescriptions are valid for Schedule III–V controlled substances.
   3. Designated Agents
      a. Can communicate a prescription for a C-III–C-V controlled substance but cannot authorize or prescribe.
      b. An authorized agent of the prescriber (employee or non-employee) may not verbally communicate emergency C-II prescriptions to a pharmacist. This task cannot be delegated.
      c. DEA requires that for non-employees of the prescriber to qualify as an agent of the prescriber, there must be a formal written appointment of the agent by the prescriber. This is important for facilities such as nursing homes where the nurses may not be employees of the physician but may wish to call in a prescription to a pharmacy on behalf of a physician.
   4. Fax prescriptions are valid for Schedule III–V controlled substances but must have the prescriber's original signature. Electronic signatures are not valid on faxed controlled substance prescriptions. Faxes for Schedule II controlled substances are only allowed in limited circumstances. *See Section VIII. B. below.*

D. Electronic Prescriptions for Controlled Substances (EPCS)
   1. DEA first authorized electronic prescriptions for controlled substances in 2010.
   2. EPCS (including Schedule II) are valid if both the prescriber's computer and the pharmacy's computer meet all DEA security requirements.
   3. Prescriber requirements include:
      a. Third-party certification of system.
      b. Credentialing to verify a provider has the authorization to prescribe controlled substances.

    c. Two-factor authentication for providers who sign an EPCS prescription.

4. Pharmacy requirements include:

    a. Third-party certification of system.

    b. Ability to sign and archive the controlled substance prescription.

    c. The system must electronically accept and store all the information that DEA requires to document the dispensing of a prescription.

    d. The system must allow the pharmacy to limit access for the annotation, alteration, or deletion of controlled substance prescriptions to specific individuals or roles.

    e. The system must have an internal audit trail that documents whenever a prescription is received, altered, annotated, or deleted.

    f. The pharmacy must conduct an internal audit daily that identifies any potential security problems, and the system must generate a report for review by the pharmacy if a problem is identified.

    g. Pharmacy systems must be backed up daily.

    h. Electronic prescription records must be kept electronically. No hard copy is required to be kept.

5. Although not a DEA rule, the comprehensive opioid bill signed into law in October 2018, the SUPPORT Act, mandated that all Medicare Part D prescriptions for controlled substances be issued electronically by January 1, 2021. The law provides exceptions for:

    a. Prescriptions issued when the practitioner and dispensing pharmacy are the same entity;

    b. Prescriptions issued that cannot be transmitted electronically under the most recently implemented version of the National Council for Prescription Drug Programs SCRIPT Standard;

    c. Prescriptions issued by a practitioner who received a waiver or a renewal thereof for a period of time as determined by CMS, not to exceed one year, due to demonstrated economic hardship, technological limitations that are not reasonably within the control of the practitioner, or other exceptional circumstances demonstrated by the practitioner;

d. Prescriptions issued by a practitioner under circumstances in which, notwithstanding the practitioner's ability to submit a prescription electronically as required, such practitioner reasonably determines that it would be impractical for the individual involved to obtain substances prescribed by electronic prescription in a timely manner, and such delay would adversely impact the individual's medical condition involved;

   e. Prescriptions issued by a practitioner prescribing a drug under a research protocol;

   f. Prescriptions issued by a practitioner for a drug for which the Food and Drug Administration requires a prescription to contain elements that are not able to be included in electronic prescribing, such as a drug with risk evaluation and mitigation strategies that include elements to assure safe use;

   g. Prescriptions issued by a practitioner for an individual who receives hospice care; and

   h. Prescriptions issued by a practitioner for an individual who is a resident of a nursing facility and dually eligible for benefits under Medicare and Medicaid.

STUDY TIP: Some states had previously mandated all controlled substance prescriptions be issued electronically, and a few states have mandated electronic prescriptions for all prescriptions including non-controlled substances. Because there are exceptions to the mandatory electronic requirements, you may still see questions regarding written and faxed controlled substance prescriptions. You should also know any exceptions to mandatory electronic prescriptions.

VIII. Schedule II Prescriptions
   A. General
   1. Schedule II prescriptions must be either written or electronically submitted.
   2. Verbal prescriptions for Schedule II drugs are not permitted except in an emergency. *See C. Emergency Dispensing of a Schedule II Controlled Substance Pursuant to a Verbal Prescription below.*
   3. Schedule II prescriptions cannot be refilled.

4. There is no time limit under federal law as to when a Schedule II prescription must be filled after being issued by the practitioner, but many state laws do place a time limit for having Schedule II prescriptions filled.

   Note: DEA does place a time limit of 30 days on the partial dispensing of Schedule II controlled substances when requested by the patient or prescriber. See D.2. below. While it makes sense that 30 days should be the time limit for getting an original Schedule II prescription filled, that is not technically how the law is written. Check your state law on this, as many states address this.

5. Changing Information or Information Omitted on a Written Schedule II Prescription.

   a. In 2022, the DEA stated they intend to write new regulations on this topic. Until then, pharmacists are permitted to adhere to state regulations or policy regarding those changes a pharmacist may make to a controlled substance after oral consultation with the prescriber.

   b. Until DEA issues new rules or guidance on this topic, you will need to check if your state has any rules or guidance. Generally, many states permit pharmacists to change items such as drug strength, dosage form, quantity, or directions for use, provided the pharmacist:

      (1) Contacts the prescribing practitioner and receives verbal permission for the change.

      (2) Documents on the prescription that the change was authorized, the name or initials of the individual granting the authorization, and the pharmacist's initials.

   c. State rules and guidelines often prohibit a pharmacist from changing the following items on a written Schedule II prescription:

      (1) Name of the patient.

      (2) Name of the drug.

      (3) Name of the prescribing physician.

      (4) Date the prescription was issued.

         Note: Some states permit calling to add a missing date or an earliest fill date. Other states do not address this, so it is sometimes unclear.

6. Quantity Limits on Schedule II Prescriptions.
   a. There is not a specific quantity limit for all Schedule II controlled substances on a single prescription under federal law.
   b. There is a 90-day supply limit when a practitioner issues multiple Schedule II prescriptions the same day. *See 7. below.*
   c. Although there is technically no quantity limit on a single controlled substance prescription under federal law, pharmacists should exercise their corresponding responsibility on every prescription to ensure it is legitimate. State laws may limit quantities on Schedule II controlled substances, or even specific categories of drugs such as opioids which may be in Schedule II but could also be in Schedule III or V.

STUDY TIP: Insurance plans or pharmacy policies may limit the amount that may be filled on a single prescription, but these are not legal requirements. Always answer MPJE questions based on legal requirements.

---

7. Multiple Prescriptions for Schedule II Drugs. (DEA Rule 21 CFR 1306.12(b)(1))
   a. DEA permits an individual practitioner to issue multiple Schedule II prescriptions on the same day, authorizing the patient to receive a total of no more than a 90-day supply of a Schedule II controlled substance. Instructions indicating the earliest fill date on which the prescriptions can be filled must be on each prescription.
   b. This 90-day supply limit only applies when the prescriber is issuing multiple prescriptions for a Schedule II controlled substance on the same day with instructions that some of the prescriptions are not to be filled until a later date.
   Note: Logically, if there is no quantity limit for a single Schedule II prescription, then there is no reason for this rule. That technically is correct, but in this case DEA realized because many insurance plans don't cover more than a 30-day supply of controlled substances, patients would need to go to the prescriber every month to get a new written prescription for any Schedule II controlled substance since they could not be called in. (This was before

electronic prescriptions were more prevalent.) Rather than having prescribers postdate a prescription, which DEA has never allowed and still does not allow, this rule was adopted. When DEA adopted this rule, they limited the total quantity to 90 days, but DEA still has not placed a days' supply limit on a single prescription for a controlled substance.

STUDY TIP: The rules for issuing multiple Schedule II prescriptions seem to cause much confusion with pharmacy students and pharmacists. Be sure you understand this concept. These are not considered refills.

   B. Facsimile Prescriptions for Schedule II Controlled Substances
      1. Facsimiles are generally not valid for Schedule II prescriptions.
      2. However, DEA recognizes three exceptions where a facsimile can serve as the original written prescription:
         a. A practitioner prescribing a Schedule II narcotic for a patient undergoing home infusion/IV pain therapy;
         b. A practitioner prescribing a Schedule II controlled substance for patients in Long Term Care Facilities (LTCFs); and
         c. A practitioner prescribing a Schedule II narcotic for a patient in hospice care.
   C. Emergency Dispensing of a Schedule II Controlled Substance Pursuant to a Verbal Prescription
      1. In an emergency situation, a practitioner may provide a verbal prescription for a Schedule II controlled substance to a pharmacy.

STUDY TIP: Communication must be from the prescriber and not a designated agent.

---

      2. Emergency means that the immediate administration of the drug is necessary for the proper treatment of the ultimate user, and that no alternative treatment is available and it is not possible for the prescribing practitioner to provide a written prescription.
      3. The quantity prescribed and dispensed is limited to the amount needed to treat the patient during the emergency period.

4. The prescription order must be immediately reduced to writing by the pharmacist and contain all information except the practitioner's signature.
5. If the prescriber is not known to the pharmacist, the pharmacist must make a reasonable effort to determine that the phone authorization came from a valid practitioner.
6. Within 7 days after authorizing an emergency telephone prescription, the prescribing practitioner must furnish the pharmacist a signed or a valid electronic prescription for the controlled substance prescribed (if mailed, it must be postmarked within 7 days). The prescription should be marked, "Authorization for Emergency Dispensing."
7. If the prescriber fails to deliver a written or electronic prescription, the pharmacist must notify the nearest DEA office.

D. Partial Dispensing of a Schedule II Controlled Substance Prescription
1. 72-Hour Rule
   a. If a pharmacist is unable to fill the entire quantity on a Schedule II controlled substance prescription, a partial quantity may be provided so long as the remaining quantity is provided within 72 hours.
   b. If the remaining quantity cannot be provided, the pharmacist must notify the prescriber.
2. 30-Day Rule
   a. Under the Comprehensive Addiction and Recovery Act (CARA) of 2016, federal law was modified in 2016 to allow partial fills of Schedule II controlled substances for up to 30 days if requested by the patient of the prescriber.
   b. The total quantity dispensed may not exceed the original quantity prescribed.
   c. This applies to written and electronic prescriptions, but not to emergency verbal Schedule II controlled substance prescriptions.

3. **60-Day Rule**
   a. For terminally ill and LTCF patients, federal law allows partial fills of Schedule II prescriptions as many times as needed as long as the partial fillings are recorded on the prescription or maintained in the pharmacy's computer system.
   b. All partial fills for terminally ill and LTCF patients must be completed within 60 days.

STUDY TIP: Be sure to understand the difference between a partial fill and a refill. Partial fills are not considered a full refill. Remember, there are no refills on a Schedule II controlled substance prescription.

IX. Schedule III–V Prescriptions
A. General Rules
   1. May be filled from written, verbal, and facsimile prescriptions.
   2. May be filled from electronic prescriptions as long as all DEA security requirements are met.
   3. May be refilled as indicated on the original prescription up to 5 times in the 6-month period from the date the prescription was issued. After 6 months, the prescription is no longer valid, even if refills remain.

STUDY TIP: There is no limit on the number of partial fills that can be provided, so long as the total amount dispensed does not exceed the total number of dosage units authorized and it is within the 6-month time period. Some pharmacy computer systems count each partial fill as a refill and invalidate the prescription after 5 partial fills, but this is not legally accurate. These prescriptions are still valid if the full quantities for all refills authorized have not been dispensed within 6 months.

B. Transfers
   1. Refills of Schedule III–V controlled substances may be transferred to another pharmacy on a onetime basis.
   2. If pharmacies share an electronic, real-time, online database of prescriptions, they may transfer up to the maximum number of refills permitted by law and the prescriber's authorization.
   3. Only refills may be transferred. By policy, DEA allows an original electronic prescription for a controlled substance (EPCS), including a Schedule II prescription, to be

transferred to another pharmacy if both pharmacies have the capability to forward and receive the EPCS using an electronic sharing program.

Note: In November 2021, DEA issued a Notice of Proposed Rulemaking to formally recognize this policy in a DEA rule. At the time of publication of this book, this rule had not been finalized.

STUDY TIP: This policy makes sense in case an electronic controlled substance prescription was transmitted to the wrong pharmacy. However, many pharmacy computer systems do not have the capability of transferring an original electronic controlled substance prescription. Also, since this is currently only allowed by DEA "policy" and is not technically in DEA's rules, pharmacies may be hesitant to do this.

C. OTC Sale of Schedule V Products
  1. The FCSA allows certain Schedule V products to be purchased from a pharmacy without a prescription.
  2. These are mainly cough suppressant products containing small amounts of codeine, such as Robitussin AC and products for diarrhea containing small amounts of opium.
  3. The total quantity which may be sold to any one purchaser within a 48-hour time period may not exceed:
    a. 240 ml (8 oz.) or 48 dosage units of products containing opium.
    b. 120 ml (4 oz.) or 24 dosage units of products containing codeine or any other controlled substance.

STUDY TIP: Many states no longer allow this, and even in states where they follow the federal law and it is technically allowed, most pharmacies do not sell these products without a prescription, but the law is still on the books in many states.

---

  4. Other requirements:
    a. Dispensing may only be made by a pharmacist and not by a non-pharmacist, even if under the supervision of a pharmacist (although after the pharmacist has made the dispensing and met recordkeeping requirements, the actual sale and delivery may be completed by a non-pharmacist).
    b. The purchaser must be at least 18 years of age and the pharmacist must require every purchaser not known to the pharmacist to provide identification and proof of age.

    c. A bound record book must be maintained by the pharmacist that contains the name and address of the purchaser, the name and quantity of the controlled substance purchased, the date of the purchase, and the name or initials of the pharmacist who dispensed the product to the purchaser.

X. Methadone, Opiate Dependence, Naloxone, and Methamphetamine Controls
  A. Prescribing and Dispensing of Certain Narcotic Drugs
    1. Methadone is used both for the treatment of severe pain and in the detoxification and maintenance of narcotic addicts in registered narcotic treatment programs.
    2. While any pharmacy can stock methadone, it can only legally be dispensed as an analgesic (for pain treatment).
    3. DEA has requested manufacturers and wholesalers to voluntarily restrict sales of methadone 40 mg to hospitals and narcotic treatment clinics only; no sales to retail pharmacies are allowed.
    4. Methadone (or any other drug) cannot be dispensed for the maintenance or detoxification of addicts unless it is provided through a registered narcotic treatment program.
    5. Narcotic treatment programs may administer and dispense (but not prescribe) narcotic drugs to a narcotic-dependent person for detoxification or maintenance treatment.
      a. Short-term detoxification means dispensing of a narcotic drug in decreasing doses for a period not to exceed 30 days.
      b. Long-term detoxification means dispensing of a narcotic drug to a narcotic-dependent person in decreasing doses in excess of 30 days but not in excess of 180 days.

STUDY TIP: Make sure you understand that a narcotic treatment program is a specific type of DEA registration that permits the administration and dispensing of methadone, but those practitioners may not write prescriptions for narcotics such as methadone for treating addiction that can be filled at a pharmacy. Pharmacies may only dispense prescriptions for methadone for pain. It is acceptable to dispense a prescription for methadone as part of a formal pain management program in which a patient is switched to methadone to control or gradually reduce dosage of other narcotics, but methadone cannot be dispensed from a pharmacy solely as a treatment for opioid dependency.

6. A physician who is not part of a narcotic treatment program may administer (not prescribe) narcotic drugs (e.g., methadone) to an addicted individual for not more than a 3-day period until the individual can be enrolled in a narcotic treatment program.

7. A hospital that is not part of a narcotic treatment program may administer narcotics to a drug-dependent person for either detoxification or maintenance therapy if the patient is being treated in the hospital for a condition other than the addiction. *Note: This may need to be done to prevent an addicted patient from going into withdrawals while in the hospital.*

B. Medication Assisted Treatment (MAT) for Opiate Dependence

STUDY TIP: The Consolidated Appropriations Act of 2023 eliminated the DATA-Waiver Program discussed below as this book was going to press. Per DEA guidance, a DATA-Waiver is no longer required to treat patients with buprenorphine for opioid use disorder, all prescriptions for buprenorphine only require a standard DEA registration, "X" codes are no longer needed, and there are no longer any limits or patient caps on the number of patients a prescriber may treat.

---

1. The Drug Addiction Treatment Act of 2000 (DATA 2000) allows office-based, specially trained practitioners to prescribe certain narcotic Schedule III–V drugs to treat opiate dependence through a risk management program outside of a narcotic treatment facility.

2. A practitioner authorized to prescribe under the Act, called a Qualifying Practitioner or a DATA-waived practitioner, can apply for a DATA 2000 waiver if they meet specific criteria. The waiver is provided by the Substance Abuse and Mental Health Services Administration (SAMHSA), and the practitioner is provided an identification or "X" code that must be included with the prescriber's DEA number. Pharmacists can verify a practitioner's DATA waiver at the SAMHSA website's Buprenorphine Pharmacy Lookup.

3. The only drugs that may be dispensed under this program are Subutex® (buprenorphine) and Suboxone® (buprenorphine/naloxone combination). These drugs, both Schedule III controlled substances, are available in sublingual form and may be dispensed by a pharmacy upon a prescription from a qualified practitioner.

4. A DATA-waived practitioner may be allowed to treat up to 30, 100, or 275 patients, depending on their authorization.

STUDY TIP: A DATA-waived practitioner can treat opioid addiction and prescribe MAT drugs (buprenorphine and buprenorphine/naloxone) from their office. They do not need to work in a Narcotic Treatment Program. Likewise, a practitioner that works in a Narcotic Treatment Program cannot automatically prescribe MAT drugs to be filled at a pharmacy. They would also need to be a DATA-waived practitioner.

---

5. In order to encourage more practitioners to seek a DATA waiver, under practice guidelines issued by SAMHSA, practitioners who limit their treatment to no more than 30 patients may apply for a waiver without having to meet certain DEA certification requirements related to training, counseling, and other ancillary services (i.e., psychosocial services) that are normally required.

6. A Qualifying Practitioner may also issue a prescription for a pharmacy to deliver a controlled substance prescribed for maintenance or detoxification treatment to a practitioner's registered location for the purpose of direct administration through either injection or implantation to a narcotic-dependent person.
   Note: This is an exception to the general rule that a prescription cannot be "for office use." Pharmacists may generally only dispense a controlled substance to an ultimate user, which includes a patient or a member of the patient's household, and may not deliver a controlled substance prescription to a practitioner. This is a limited exception to that and is only for controlled substances administered through injection or implantation, so it would not be for sublingual buprenorphine or buprenorphine/naloxone.

C. The Combat Methamphetamine Epidemic Act of 2005
   1. This law was passed by Congress to further control the sale of OTC products containing precursor chemicals used in the illicit manufacturing of methamphetamine.
   2. The law classifies all products (including multiple-ingredient products) containing ephedrine, pseudoephedrine, and phenylpropanolamine as "listed chemical products."
   Note: Since this law was passed, ephedrine and phenylpropanolamine products have all been removed from the market

by FDA, so the law really only impacts pseudoephedrine products.

3. Products containing a "listed chemical" are subject to the following requirements:

   a. Display Restrictions—Although the products may be sold by any retailer, covered products must be placed behind a counter (not necessarily a pharmacy counter) or, if located on the selling floor, in a locked cabinet.

   b. Retail Sales Limits—Sales of covered products to an individual are limited to 3.6 g of the base product per day and 9 g of the base product per 30 days. Many states have sales limits per transaction.

   c. For pseudoephedrine HCL, the daily limit of 3.6 g of base product equals:

   (1) 146 of the 30 mg tablets.

   (2) 73 of the 60 mg tablets.

   (3) 36 of the 120 mg tablets.

   Note: The 2022 edition of the DEA Pharmacists Manual states that these quantity limits also apply to prescriptions for pseudoephedrine products. This is a reversal of 15 years of not requiring these limits when the drugs are prescribed pursuant to a valid prescription and the tracking systems in pharmacies do not currently capture prescription quantities. Pharmacy groups are asking DEA to reverse this interpretation

   d. Product Packaging—Covered products (other than liquids including gel caps) must either be in blister or unit-dose packaging.

4. Recordkeeping Requirements:

   a. Retailer must maintain an electronic or written logbook that identifies the products by name, quantity sold, names and addresses of purchasers, and dates and times of sales.

   b. There is an exception for the logbook requirement for individual sales of a single "convenience" package of less than 60 mg of pseudoephedrine.

   c. Purchaser must present a photo identification issued by a state or federal government, must sign the logbook, and enter his or her name, address, and date and time of sale.

    d. Retailer must verify that the name entered in the log-book corresponds to the customer identification.

    5. Employee Training:
        a. Employers certify that employees who deal directly with customers have undergone training to ensure they understand the requirements of the law.
        b. DEA requirements for self-certification and training can be found at *www.deadiversion.usdoj.gov/meth/index .html.*
    6. Mail-Service Limitations:
        a. Mail-service companies must confirm the identity of purchasers.
        b. Sales are limited to 7.5 g per 30-day period.
    7. Mobile Retail Vendors ("flea markets"):
        a. Product must be placed in a locked cabinet.
        b. Sales are limited to no more than 7.5 g of base product per customer per 30 days.

XI. Prescription Monitoring Programs (PMPs)
  A. General Information
    1. Although there are not federal laws for Prescription Monitoring Programs, they are being covered here because they are such an important aspect of controlled substance laws and pharmacy practice.
    2. Prescription monitoring programs (PMPs) or Prescription Drug Monitoring Programs (PDMPs) are an important tool in preventing the illegitimate prescribing and dispensing of controlled substances.
    3. Studies suggest that PMPs improve patient safety and reduce the risk of overdose by identifying patients at risk of abuse, reducing inappropriate prescribing and preventing patient "doctor shopping" and "pharmacy shopping" (the practice of obtaining prescriptions from multiple providers and filling those prescriptions at multiple pharmacies).
    4. PMPs are electronic databases that collect data on controlled substance prescriptions prescribed and dispensed in a state.

5. More states have begun to make checking the PMP mandatory before a practitioner can prescribe and before a pharmacy can dispense controlled substances or sometimes certain controlled substances. This has become easier to do as these systems have become integrated into electronic health record systems for prescribers and pharmacy computer systems for pharmacists. Even when checking that the PMP is mandatory, there are often exceptions. Make sure you are familiar with any of those exceptions.

6. Many of the PMP systems now provide for automated alerts based on specific criteria. These are unsolicited reports sent to prescribers or pharmacies based on questionable activity by a patient. PMPs also offer advanced analytics, machine-learning risk scores, and more to help physicians and pharmacists assess a patient's risk. This may include scoring systems assessing controlled substance usage and overdose risk.

7. The requirements of PMPs vary by state, so you will need to research the details of the program in your state. Be sure to review:
   a. Is checking the PMP mandatory?
   b. If so, is it required for all controlled substances or only certain schedules or drug classes?
   c. How often must dispensing information be reported to the PMP?
   d. What information is required to be transmitted to the PMP?
   e. Are zero reports required if a pharmacy does not dispense any controlled substances during a specified time period?
   f. What are the confidentiality and security requirements for the PMP, and who is allowed access to the PMP?

CHAPTER FOUR
United States Pharmacopeia (USP) Chapters

This chapter was written by
Patricia Kienle, R.Ph., MPA, BCSCP, FASHP

Patricia Kienle is the Director of Accreditation and Medication Safety for Cardinal Health. She received her pharmacy degree from the Philadelphia College of Pharmacy and Science and a Masters in Public Administration from Marywood University in Scranton, Pennsylvania. She is Board Certified as a Sterile Compounding Pharmacist, completed an Executive Fellowship in Patient Safety from Virginia Commonwealth University in Richmond, Virginia, and is an Adjunct Clinical Faculty member at Wilkes University in Wilkes-Barre, Pennsylvania.

She served on the Board of Directors of the American Society of Health-System Pharmacists and as President of the Pennsylvania Society of Hospital Pharmacists. She is a Fellow of ASHP, was named Pharmacist of the Year by PSHP, and is the recipient of the Distinguished Achievement Award in Hospital and Institutional Practice from the American Pharmaceutical Association Academy of Pharmacy Practice and Management, the Distinguished Leadership Award from ASHP, the ASHP John W. Webb Lecture Award, and the Thomas S. Foster Award from the United States Pharmacopeia. She has served on the Pharmacotherapy Specialty Council of the Board of Pharmacy Specialties, the Pennsylvania Patient Safety Authority, the Hospital Professional and Technical Advisory Committee of The Joint Commission, and on the Board of Governors of the National Patient Safety Foundation. She is a current member of the USP Compounding Expert Committee and chairs the Subcommittee on Hazardous Drugs.

Patti is the author of Compounding Sterile Preparations: ASHP's Visual Guide to Chapter 797, *co-author of* Meeting Accreditation Standards: A

Pharmacy Preparation Guide, *and author of* The Chapter 795 Answer Book, The Chapter 797 Answer Book, *and* The Chapter 800 Answer Book.

With over 500 invited presentations and 80 publications, she has special interests in promoting medication safety, compounding sterile preparations, accreditation, and regulatory issues.

CHAPTER FOUR
United States Pharmacopeia (USP) Chapters

This chapter provides an overview of the primary USP Chapters dealing with pharmacy compounding. MPJE Competency statement 4.5 covers compounding of sterile, nonsterile, hazardous, and non-hazardous substances, and compounding questions are frequently asked on the MPJE. USP Chapters 795 (nonsterile), 797 (sterile), and 800 (hazardous drugs) are the USP Chapters most frequently adopted by states regarding compounding. Some states have adopted these Chapters by reference and other states have adopted modified versions of these Chapters or may not have adopted them at all. You will need to review your state law for any differences, but these summaries should be helpful for you to prepare for the MPJE.

I. Introduction
A. Legal recognition
1. USP sets standards for identity, strength, quality, and purity of medications. The standards are published in the United States Pharmacopeia-National Formulary (USP-NF) compendium.
2. USP standards are recognized in the Federal Food, Drug, and Cosmetic Act (FDCA) and in various state laws and regulations. USP Chapters are considered "compendially applicable," meaning they are enforceable under federal regulations when they are numbered under 1000, and they are referenced in a General Notice, monograph, or another chapter numbered under 1000.

STUDY TIP: When standards use the terms "must" or "shall," it is a requirement. When standards use the term "should," it is a recommendation.

B. USP Components
1. USP General Notices provide basic information for use of the standards, such as descriptions of dosage forms, temperature requirements, and other information.
2. USP General Chapters contain established procedures, methods, and practices. USP 795, 797, and 800 are examples of General Chapters.

3. USP Monographs contain specific information about a formulation or compound. The *USP Compounding Compendium* contains 240 different compounding monographs.
4. Monographs are more specific than General Chapters. General Chapters are more specific than General Notices. When information conflicts, the more specific document applies.

C. Enforcement
1. USP does not enforce the standards. Enforcement is accomplished by states and by accreditation organizations that incorporate the standards into their requirements.
2. The FDCA mandates use of USP standards for compounding. When bulk drug substances (active pharmaceutical ingredients, or APIs) are used, those APIs must comply with the standards in a USP monograph (if one exists) and the applicable USP compounding standard (795 for nonsterile compounding or 797 for sterile compounding).
3. The 2013 Drug Quality and Security Act (DQSA) reaffirmed USP's authority over compounding in Section 503A. This Act distinguishes 503A entities (compounding pharmacies which supply patient-specific preparations) from 503B entities (outsourcing facilities which supply non-patient-specific preparations). Generally, 503A pharmacies are governed by state boards and follow USP compounding chapters. 503B outsourcing facilities are governed by the Food and Drug Administration (FDA) and must comply with more stringent current Good Manufacturing Practices (cGMPs).

D. Compounding
1. The FDA exempts compounding from the rigorous requirements for a new drug application, provided the compound is made by a licensed pharmacist or physician and complies with the USP Chapters on pharmacy compounding. The FDA also provides other guidance documents related to compounding.
2. States define compounding in their pharmacy rules and regulations.
3. Four General Chapters provide compounding information.
   a. USP 795 Pharmaceutical Compounding—Nonsterile Preparations
   b. USP 797 Pharmaceutical Compounding—Sterile Preparations

    c. USP 800 Hazardous Drugs—Compounding in Health-care Settings

    d. USP 825 Radiopharmaceuticals—Preparation, Compounding, Dispensing, and Repackaging
      Note: USP 825 is not covered in this book.

II. USP 795 Pharmaceutical Compounding—Nonsterile Preparations

The 2014 version of USP Chapter 795 is the official chapter through October 31, 2023. The revision of Chapter 795 published on November 1, 2022, will become official on November 1, 2023. Section II. highlights the currently official (2014) version.

A. Introduction and Scope

    1. Chapter 795 provides minimal standards for compounding nonsterile formulations (Compounded Nonsterile Preparations, CNSPs) for human and animal patients. It guides the compounder in practices to ensure CNSPs have the strength, quality, and purity intended.

    2. Chapter 795 applies to all healthcare personnel who compound CNSPs.

    3. Applicable federal and state laws and regulations concerning compounding must also be followed.

    4. If hazardous drugs are compounded, both USP 795 and USP 800 (*Hazardous Drugs—Handling in Healthcare Settings*) apply. The Occupational Safety and Health Administration (OSHA) and the National Institute for Occupational Safety and Health (NIOSH) have additional guidance concerning hazardous drugs.

STUDY TIP: Federal laws and regulations include those promulgated by agencies such as the Food and Drug Administration (FDA) and Centers for Medicare and Medicaid Services (CMS). State agencies include state boards of pharmacy and health. Accreditation organizations such as The Joint Commission and the Pharmacy Compounding Accreditation Board (PCAB) may also include USP standards in their requirements.

B. Categories of compounding

    1. Simple compounding includes preparation of CNSPs according to USP monographs, use of manufacturer's information to reconstitute a commercial product, or following the complete directions in a peer-reviewed journal.

2. Moderate compounding includes preparations requiring special calculations or procedures or mixing a CNSP for which the stability data is not known.
3. Complex compounding includes preparing CNSPs that require special procedures or equipment.
4. The categories of compounding do not affect the assignment of beyond-use dates (BUDs) for nonsterile compounds.

STUDY TIP: Examples of types of compounding include:
- Simple—reconstituting an amoxicillin suspension according to the manufacturer's instructions.
- Moderate—mixing two ointments for which stability information is not available.
- Complex—preparing a transdermal dosage form.

C. Responsibilities of compounders
   1. USP 795 uses the term "compounders" to mean both the person supervising compounding and personnel who compound CNSPs.
   2. The compounder is responsible for preparing CNSPs of intended strength, quality, and purity.
   3. Training.
      a. Compounders must be trained and able to demonstrate competence for assigned activities.
      b. The supervisor must demonstrate procedures to the compounder, who must then perform the compounding for the supervisor.
      c. All training must be documented.
      d. Compounders should document competency at least annually.
D. Facilities
   1. A dedicated compounding area must be defined and limited to authorized personnel. The area must be clean, orderly, and sanitary.
   2. Temperature and ventilation control must be adequate.

STUDY TIP: No specific temperature and humidity is listed in USP 795, but the drugs stored in the area must meet applicable USP and FDA requirements.

---

3. Space for orderly placement of equipment, ingredients, and other components must be available.
4. Compounding CNSPs made with hazardous drugs must also follow the requirements in USP 800 to protect the patient, compounder, and environment.
5. Compounding for sterile preparations must follow the requirements of USP 797.
6. The compounding area must have a source of potable water for washing equipment and performing hand hygiene.
7. Sinks for hand and equipment washing and other devices (e.g., dishwasher) must be accessible to the compounding area.
8. The plumbing system must be free of defects that could compromise the CNSP.
9. Appropriate waste containers must be available, and proper handling and disposal must be done.

STUDY TIP: Some states have specific requirements, including limitation of use of the area, minimum square footage, etc.

10. Equipment
    a. Equipment must be clean, properly maintained, and intended for use for compounding.
    b. Purified water should be used for rinsing equipment and other devices (e.g., spatulas, glassware) used in compounding.

STUDY TIP: There is no requirement in the 2008 version of USP 795 to compound preparations in a powder containment hood, but many pharmacies use this device to avoid contaminating themselves or cross-contaminating CNSPs when powders or drugs that aerosolize are manipulated.

E. Hand Hygiene, Garb, and Personal Protective Equipment (PPE)
    1. Compounders' clothing must be clean and suitable for the type of compounding performed.
    2. Hand hygiene (i.e., hand washing) must be performed as detailed in the organization's policy.
    3. Garb and PPE include hair covers, face masks, gloves, gowns, and shoe covers. Additional PPE is required when compounding hazardous drugs (HDs).

F. Standard Operating Procedures (SOPs) and Other Documentation
   1. SOPs.
      a. The person in charge of compounding needs to establish and maintain adequate policies and procedures to ensure safe and reproducible CNSPs. SOPs should include details concerning facilities, equipment, personnel, receipt, storage, compounding, and other related elements.
      b. When errors or other excursions occur, policies should guide the process to identify and correct the occurrence.
   2. Safety Data Sheets (SDS).
   Safety Data Sheets (formerly called Material Safety Data Sheets, or MSDS) must be available to personnel working with bulk chemicals or other specific drugs.
   3. A Master Formulation Record (MFR) must be created for each CNSP. The MFR must include:
      a. Official name, strength, and dosage form.
      b. Calculations needed.
      c. Description of all ingredients and their amounts.
      d. References for compatibility and stability.
      e. Equipment needed.
      f. Mixing instructions.
      g. Labeling information.
      h. Container to use for dispensing.
      i. Packaging and storage requirements.
      j. Description of the final CNSP.
      k. Quality control procedures and expected results.
   4. A Compounding Record (CR) must be created each time a CNSP is mixed. The CR must include:
      a. Official or assigned name, strength, and dosage.
      b. MFR reference.
      c. Names and quantities of all components.
      d. Total quantity compounded.
      e. Names of personnel who compounded, performed quality control, and approved the CNSP.
      f. Date of preparation.
      g. Assigned BUD.
      h. Copy of the label.
      i. Description of the final CNSP.

j. Results of quality control procedures.

k. Documentation of any quality control excursions or other problems reported by the patient or caregiver.

    5. Records must be retained for the time required for prescriptions in state regulations.

G. Ingredients

    1. Ingredients (sometimes called "components") of a CNSP include:

        a. Active Pharmaceutical Ingredient (API), the ingredient that provides the pharmacological activity of the CNSP.

        b. Vehicle, such as the diluent used.

        c. Added substances, an inactive ingredient in the CNSP (sometimes called the "excipient").

    2. Ingredients must be obtained from reliable sources and stored according to manufacturer's information and applicable laws and regulations. When possible, ingredients meeting standards of the United States Pharmacopeia (USP), National Formulary (NF), or Food Chemicals Codex (FCC) should be used. Ingredients should be obtained from FDA-registered facilities when possible.

    3. Ingredients must be stored appropriately and cannot be stored on the floor. Ingredients that have a manufacturer's or supplier's expiration date may be used through that date as long as the container is stored to avoid decomposition of the contents. If no expiration date is provided, the compounder must assign a date that is no longer than three years from the date of receipt.

    4. Active Pharmaceutical Ingredients (APIs) are the raw powders (sometimes called "bulk substances") used for compounding. Applicable Safety Data Sheets (SDS) and other required documentation must be available for compounders.

5. APIs that are not USP or NF grade must be accompanied by a lot-specific Certificate of Analysis (COA).

6. Ingredients used for compounding CNSPs for humans must not be those that have been withdrawn from the market for safety purposes.

7. Ingredients used for compounding CNSPs for food-producing animals must not be on the federal list of components prohibited. If an ingredient is derived from a ruminant animal (e.g., bovine, caprine, ovine), the supplier must provide written information that the ingredient is in compliance with laws and regulations for the component.

8. Weighing, measuring, and mixing of ingredients must be performed and verified to be sure the CNSP contains the expected qualities.

9. When water is included in a CNSP, purified water must be used.

H. Compounding

1. Any CNSP mixed must be evaluated for suitability and safety, including evaluation of properties of the CNSP, dosage form, appropriateness for use, and legal limitations.

2. Compounding must be limited to one preparation at a time in a specific workspace.

3. Assignment of beyond-use dates (BUDs).

   a. The BUD is the date beyond which a CNSP must not be used.

   b. The CNSP must maintain purity, potency/strength, quality, and expected characteristics through the BUD assigned.

STUDY TIP: Expiration dates are provided by manufacturers for their products. BUDs are established by compounders for their preparations.

---

   c. For CNSPs that do not have stability information for the specific formulation (including drug, diluent, container, and closure), the compounder must limit the BUDs assigned to the following:

Type of Formulation	Maximum BUD
Water-containing oral formulation	14 days (*refrigerated*)
Water-containing topical/dermal and mucosal liquid and semisolid formulations	30 days
Nonaqueous formulations	6 months

    d. BUDs may be extended beyond the default dates above if stability studies of the formulation are conducted with appropriate results, or if a USP monograph is followed exactly and contains a longer BUD.

    e. The BUD cannot be longer than the expiration date of any of its components.

  4. Labeling.

    a. CNSPs must be labeled as detailed in the Master Formulation Record and include all elements required by laws and regulations.

    b. CNSP labels should include: "This is a compounded preparation."

    c. Labels of CNSPs for food-producing animals must include the withdrawal time (WDT) provided by the veterinarian. The WDT indicates the length of time that animal tissue of food-producing animals cannot be used for human food supply.

I. Dispensing

  1. All applicable laws and regulations must be followed when dispensing CNSPs.

  2. Packaging must meet USP requirements.

  3. Appropriate consultation should be provided to the patient or caregiver.

J. Quality control and final check of CNSPs

  1. The compounder must compare the elements of the CNSP (e.g., weight, clarity, color, odor, consistency, pH, other testing as required) to the Master Formulation Record.

  2. The CNSP must be packaged as detained in the Master Formulation Record.

  3. A method to recall CNSPs must be developed in case that action is necessary.

III. Highlights of 2023 Revision of USP 795 Pharmaceutical Compounding—Nonsterile Preparations

Note: The 2023 revision of USP Chapter 795 becomes effective November 1, 2023, and it may be even longer before states adopt these changes into their regulations. This means it is unlikely you will see questions on these changes on the MPJE during 2023. The following summary is intended to highlight the upcoming changes to USP Chapter 795.

A. Categories of nonsterile compounding previously listed in Chapter 795 have been eliminated.

B. Compounding of nonsterile hazardous drugs must also follow requirements in USP Chapter 800—Hazardous Drugs: Handling in Healthcare Settings.

C. Compounding of nonsterile radiopharmacuticals must also follow requirements in USP Chapter 825—Radiopharmceuticals: Preparation, Compounding, Dispensing, and Repackaging.

D. Preparation following manufacturer's instructions (such as reconstituting an FDA-approved antibiotic suspension) is out of the scope of Chapter 795, provided it is limited to a single patient.

E. A designated person is required to oversee compounding activities.

F. Gloves are required to be worn when compounding.

G. If weighing, measuring, or other activities that could create airborne particle are performed, the pharmacy needs to evaluate the need for containment of the particles.

H. Compounds must be evaluated for water activity, since beyond-use dates are based on the potential for water to affect the stability of the preparation.

IV. USP 797 Pharmaceutical Compounding—Sterile Preparations
The 2008 version of USP Chapter 797 is the official chapter through October 31, 2023. The revision of Chapter 797 published on November 1, 2022, will become official on November 1, 2023. Section IV. highlights the currently official (2008) version.

A. Introduction and Scope

    1. Chapter 797 provides standards to prevent harm that could occur from microbial, chemical, or physical contamination; incorrect strength; or inappropriate quality of compounded sterile preparations (CSPs) for human and animal patients.

    2. Chapter 797 applies to all healthcare personnel who compound CNSPs and applies in all healthcare settings.

    3. CSPs include drugs and biologics such as injections, infusions, irrigations for wounds and body cavities, ophthalmics (including drops), tissue implants, baths and soaks for organs and tissues, aqueous bronchial and nasal inhalations, and other preparations intended to be sterile.

4. Applicable state and federal laws and regulations concerning compounding must also be followed.
5. If hazardous drugs are compounded, both USP 797 and USP 800 (*Hazardous Drugs—Handling in Healthcare Settings*) apply. The Occupational Safety and Health Administration (OSHA) and the National Institute for Occupational Safety and Health (NIOSH) have additional guidance concerning hazardous drugs.
6. USP 797 has sections concerning the special requirements for preparation of allergen extracts and radiopharmaceuticals. The radiopharmaceutical information is now supplemented by a new USP Chapter: USP 825 *Radiopharmaceuticals—Preparation, Compounding, Dispensing, and Repackaging.*

STUDY TIP: Federal laws and regulations include those promulgated by agencies such as the Food and Drug Administration (FDA) and Centers for Medicare and Medicaid Services (CMS). State agencies include state boards of pharmacy and health. Accreditation organizations such as The Joint Commission and the Pharmacy Compounding Accreditation Board (PCAB) may also include USP standards in their requirements.

B. Categories of CSPs
1. Immediate Use preparations are those mixed outside of the facilities described in the chapter when the urgency does not permit mixing in a cleanroom suite or segregated compounding area (SCA). Immediate Use preparations are limited to simple transfer of not more than 3 sterile manufactured ingredients and not more than 2 entries into any one container.
2. Low Risk CSPs are those mixed in a USP 797–compliant area as a single dose for one patient.
3. Medium Risk CSPs are those mixed in a USP 797–compliant area as a batch for multiple patients or for one patient on multiple occasions, or more complex mixtures such as Total Parenteral Nutrition (TPN) solutions.
4. High Risk CSPs are those mixed in a USP 797–compliant cleanroom suite with a nonsterile starting ingredient, or any risk level if mixed without complete garb as required.
5. The risk levels are key elements in determining the beyond-use dates (BUDs) for sterile compounds.

C. Responsibilities of compounders
   1. The compounder is responsible for preparing CSPs that are accurately mixed, within 10% of labeled strength/potency (unless otherwise listed), and prepared with appropriate technique in proper facilities.
   2. Training
      a. Compounders must be trained and able to demonstrate competence for assigned activities.
      b. Initial training includes theoretical principles, practical skills including aseptic work practices, observation of expert compounders, return demonstrations, and successful completion of written competences, hand hygiene and garbing, a gloved fingertip test without any contamination, and media fill tests.
      c. Requalifying training includes successful completion of written tests, media fill tests, and requalifying gloved fingertip tests. The media fill tests and requalifying glove fingertip tests must be done at least every 6 months if high-risk CSPs are mixed, or at least every 12 months if only low- and medium-risk CSPs are mixed.
      d. Media fill tests must mimic the most complex CSP mixed. A successful media fill test is one that shows no growth or cloudiness over the time period of the test.
      e. Gloved fingertip tests are done at initial training (to check for the ability to aseptically garb) and as a requalifying test at the same frequency as required for media fill tests.

      f. All training must be documented.

D. Facilities

    1. The sterile compounding area must be properly designed with cleanable surfaces and should have a temperature under 20°C. No humidity requirement is listed in the 2008 version of USP 795, but the relative humidity should be under 60%. Some states have specific requirements.

    2. Primary Engineering Controls

        a. Primary Engineering Controls (PECs, informally called *hoods*) are the devices in which CSPs are mixed.

        b. Laminar air flow workbenches (LAFWs) and biological safety cabinets (BSCs) are examples of traditional types of PECs.

        c. Compounding aseptic isolators (CAIs) and compounding aseptic containment isolators (CACIs) are examples of compounding isolators.

        d. PECs must meet specific criteria, including maintenance of an ISO 5 classification, have unidirectional air flow, and meet other requirements listed in USP 797.

STUDY TIP: ISO class is determined by the number of particles larger than 0.5 microns in a volume of air. The smaller the ISO number, the cleaner the air. PECs must be ISO 5 or cleaner. Anterooms that open into a negative pressure room and buffer rooms must be ISO 7 or cleaner. Anterooms that open only into positive pressure buffer rooms must be ISO 8 or cleaner.

---

    3. Secondary Engineering Controls

        a. Secondary Engineering Controls (SECs, informally called the IV room or IV lab) are the rooms in which the PEC is placed.

        b. USP 797 details specific requirements including ISO classification, pressurization, air flow, and other characteristics.

        c. There are two types of SECs:

            (1) A cleanroom suite, consisting of a positive pressure anteroom and at least one buffer room. The anteroom must be positive pressure and must be at least ISO 7 if it opens into any negative pressure buffer room, or at least ISO 8 if it opens only into positive pressure buffer rooms. The buffer room must be at least ISO 7.

            (2) A segregated compounding area (SCA), which is an area designated for use for sterile compounding. It does not have to be a separate room, but that is preferred. A more complex containment segregated compounding area (C-SCA) is used for compounding hazardous drugs. *See Section IV. on USP 800 below for details.*

SEC	Minimum ISO Classification
Anteroom that opens only into positive pressure buffer room(s)	ISO 8
Anteroom that opens into one or more negative pressure room(s)	ISO 7
Positive pressure buffer room	ISO 7
Negative pressure buffer room	ISO 7
Segregated Compounding Area	Not required to be ISO-classified
Containment Segregated Compounding Area	Not required to be ISO-classified

STUDY TIP: Some states have specific requirements, including limitation of use of the area, minimum square footage, etc.

4. Pressure gradients between rooms in a sterile compounding suite minimize the possibility of microbial contamination.
   a. The buffer room (where the hood is placed) must be 0.020" more positive than the anteroom.
   b. The anteroom must be 0.020" more positive than the general area it opens into.
   c. There is no pressure gradient requirement for SCAs.
   d. There is a negative pressure requirement for hazardous drug ("chemo") buffer rooms and C-SCAs. *See Section IV. on USP 800 below for details.*

5. Current (2008) USP 797 allows a clean room that is a single room with an ante area and a buffer area. A line dividing the two areas must be used to demonstrate air flow of 40 feet per minute from the buffer to ante area. This design is not recommended and is unlikely to be allowed in the future.

6. Other devices and equipment.
   a. The cleanroom suite or SCA must be designed to promote proper cleaning. Sinks, counters, pass-throughs, refrigerators, and other equipment and devices must be suitable for use in the IV room, properly placed, and cleaned.

    b. Devices specifically designed for use in the PEC, such as automated compounding devices (ACDs) and repeater pumps, must be used according to manufacturer's instructions and only by compounders who have been assessed for competence.

  7. Certification—PECs and SECs must be certified every 6 months by a qualified certification technician.

E. Hand Hygiene, Garb, and Personal Protective Equipment (PPE)

  1. Hand hygiene (i.e., hand washing) must be performed as detailed in the organization's policy. Hands and forearms must be washed with soap and water up to elbows for 30 seconds.

  2. Garb and PPE includes hair covers, face masks, gloves, gowns, and shoe covers. Additional PPE is required when compounding hazardous drugs (HDs).

  3. There is a specific order in which to don garb and perform hand hygiene:

    a. Don head and hair covers, masks, and shoe covers upon entry to the anteroom or SCA.

    b. In an anteroom, step over into the clean side of the room.

    c. Perform hand hygiene.

    d. Don gown.

    e. Apply alcohol-based hand rub to hands and allow to dry.

    f. Don sterile gloves.

F. Standard Operating Procedures (SOPs) and Other Documentation

  1. Standard Operating Procedures (SOPs).

    a. The person in charge of compounding needs to establish and maintain adequate policies and procedures to ensure safe and reproducible CNSPs. SOPs should include details concerning facilities, equipment, personnel, receipt, storage, compounding, and other related elements.

    b. When errors or other excursions occur, policies should guide the process to identify and correct the occurrence.

  2. Master Formulation Records and Compounding Records are not required in the 2008 version of USP 797, but similar records are necessary. Some states require all the elements listed for the MFRs and CRs in USP 795 and in the proposed revision to USP 797 that was published in 2019. In any case, appropriate records should be developed and maintained, such as logs for batches of CSPs made.

G. Compounding Technique

    1. Aseptic technique is a core practice that must be mastered.

    2. Maintaining sterility of critical sites is essential. Critical sites are areas such as vial septa, ports, needle hubs, and other surfaces at highest risk of exposure to contamination.

H. Components

    1. Ingredients must be obtained from reliable sources and stored according to manufacturer's information and applicable laws and regulations. When possible, ingredients meeting standards of the United States Pharmacopeia (USP), National Formulary (NF), or Food Chemicals Codex (FCC) should be used. Ingredients should be obtained from FDA-registered facilities when possible.

    2. Ingredients must be stored appropriately and cannot be stored on the floor. Ingredients that have a manufacturer's or supplier's expiration date may be used through that date as long as the container is stored to avoid decomposition of the contents. If no expiration date is provided, the compounder must assign a date that is no longer than one year from the date of receipt, unless testing proves it has retained the purity and quality required.

    3. Active Pharmaceutical Ingredients (APIs) are the raw powders (sometimes called "bulk substances") used for compounding. Applicable Safety Data Sheets (SDS) and other required documentation must be available for compounders.

    4. APIs that are not USP or NF grade must be accompanied by a lot-specific Certificate of Analysis (COA).

    5. Ingredients used for compounding CSPs for humans must not be those that have been withdrawn from the market for safety purposes.

I. Compounding process

    1. Most CSPs are mixed using only conventionally manufactured sterile components. The goal for sterile-to-sterile compounding is to maintain sterility.

    2. High-risk CSPs are mixed using nonsterile starting ingredients. The goal for nonsterile-to-sterile compounding is to achieve sterility. Sterilization of the final CSP is achieved using terminal sterilization (such as in an autoclave using steam under pressure) or by filtration. Both methods require quality control measures to ensure they have performed as intended.

a. Autoclaving is monitored using biological indicators.

b. Filtration is checked by performing a bubble point test of the used filter to ensure its integrity.

STUDY TIP: Terminal sterilization is described in USP 797 as by use of an autoclave (steam under pressure) or dry heat. Filtration is not terminal sterilization.

---

3. High-risk CSPs (except those for inhalation or ophthalmic administration) that are made in groups of more than 25 units must also pass a bacterial endotoxin (pyrogen) test.

4. Components used for preparation of CSPs have limited inuse times:

Type of component	Allowable in-use time when opened in and maintained in ISO 5	Allowable in-use time when opened outside of or removed from ISO 5
Ampule	Use and discard remainder	Use and discard remainder
Single-dose vial	Up to 6 hours	Up to 1 hour
Multiple-dose vial	Up to 28 days (unless manufacturer's instructions differ)	Up to 28 days (unless manufacturer's instructions differ)

5. Assignment of beyond-use dates (BUDs).

a. The BUD is the date beyond which a CSP must not be used.

STUDY TIP: Expiration dates are provided by manufacturers for their products. BUDs are established by compounders for their preparations.

---

b. BUDs for CSPs that do not have stability information for the specific formulation (including drug, diluent, container, and closure) must limit the BUDs assigned to the following:

Category	Stored at controlled room temperature	Stored under refrigeration	Stored frozen
Immediate Use	1 hour	Not applicable	Not applicable
Low Risk made in an SCA	12 hours	12 hours	Not applicable
Low Risk	48 hours	14 days	45 days
Medium Risk	30 hours	9 days	45 days
High Risk	24 hours	3 days	45 days

    c. BUDs may be extended beyond the default dates above if stability studies of the formulation are conducted with appropriate results or if a USP monograph is followed exactly and contains a longer BUD.

    d. The BUD cannot be longer than the expiration date of any of its components.

  6. Labeling.

Labels of CSPs must include the drug name and strength/concentration, total volume, BUD, route of administration, and storage conditions. Other information to support safe use, organizational policy, and state laws and regulations must be included as appropriate.

J. Dispensing the Final Preparation

  1. The compounder must check the final CSP prior to dispensing. Identification of the individual who checked the final CSP must be documented.

  2. Many CSPs require storage at refrigerator temperature if not immediately dispensed. Those CSPs that will be shipped to a location other than where they are compounded (e.g., to a patient's home) must have appropriate temperature control.

K. Cleaning the Compounding Areas

  1. Solutions used must be appropriate for use in a cleanroom and (if necessary) properly diluted. Many solutions have a "dwell time," which is the time the solution needs to be wet and in contact with the surface in order to achieve its intended result (e.g., decontamination, cleaning, disinfection).

  2. Cleaning PECs and SECs is done with a detergent. After cleaning, the PEC needs to have sterile 70% isopropyl alcohol applied to the surface of the PEC.

  3. The PEC surface must be cleaned at the beginning of each shift, before each batch, every 30 minutes during compounding, after spills, and when surface contamination is known or suspected.

  4. Floors, counters, and other easily cleanable surfaces (e.g., refrigerator handles, pass-through chambers) must be cleaned daily.

5. Storage shelving, walls, and ceilings must be cleaned at least monthly.
6. Only compounding personnel can clean the PECs, but some organizations allow others with documented competency to clean floors, walls, and ceilings.

L. Environmental Monitoring
1. Environmental monitoring consists of nonviable (e.g., temperature, pressure gradients, air flow) and viable (microbial contamination) elements.
2. Some nonviable parameters must be monitored daily by compounding personnel:
    a. Temperature of the compounding areas, which should be 20°C or lower to minimize the risk of microbial contamination and for the comfort of the garbed compounder. If drugs are stored in the compounding area, the required temperature range for the drugs must be maintained.
    b. Pressure gradients between rooms. USP 797 requires minimum pressure gradients between rooms. Positive pressure rooms assist in preventing contamination entering the room, so are used for anterooms and nonhazardous buffer rooms. Negative pressure rooms assist in containing hazards, so are used for hazardous ("chemo") buffer rooms.

Between	Minimum pressure gradient required
Nonhazardous buffer room to anteroom	Buffer room must be at least 0.020" more positive than the anteroom
Hazardous buffer room to anteroom	Buffer room must be between 0.010 and 0.030" negative to anteroom
Anteroom to adjacent general area	Anteroom must be at least 0.020" more positive than general area
Segregated Compounding Area	No requirement
Containment Segregated Compounding Area to adjacent general area	C-SCA must be between 0.010 to 0.030" negative to adjacent area

STUDY TIP: Be sure to know the minimum pressure gradients required between areas.

  c. Combined ante/buffer rooms must have a displacement air flow of at least 40 feet per minute over the line of demarcation from the buffer area to the ante area.

3. Certification.

Certification involves a qualified technician checking and ensuring that nonviable parameters listed in USP 797 (e.g., particle counts, air flow, proper pressurization, and other elements) are within manufacturer's and industry specifications. PECs must be certified every six months and after servicing. SECs must be certified every six months or when changes are made in the room that could affect the air flow.

4. Viable monitoring.

  a. The facilities in which low-, medium-, and high-risk CSPs are made must be monitored to ensure microbial (bacterial and fungal) contaminants are not present to a degree that could harm patients.

  b. Viable monitoring is accomplished with electronic air sampling and surface sampling.

  c. Electronic air sampling must be checked at least every 6 months. Surface sampling must be checked periodically. Most organizations have their certifiers perform this sampling. Many organizations supplement these semiannual checks with additional sampling. Facilities that mix only low- and medium-risk-level CSPs must test for bacteria; facilities mixing high-risk-level CSPs must test for bacteria and fungus. However, most organizations test for both bacteria and fungus, even if they mix only low- and medium-risk CSPs.

  d. Action Levels based on the maximum number of CFUs allowed are listed in USP 797. If the action levels are exceeded or if trends are noted, the compounder needs to consult with a trained microbiologist to develop a remedial plan. Organisms exceeding the action level should be identified at least to the genus level. Highly pathogenic organisms (e.g., gram-negative rods, coagulase positive staphylococcus, molds, and yeasts) must be immediately remedied even if they do not exceed the action level.

Action Levels in Number of Colony Forming Units (CFUs)		
ISO Classification	Air Sample (per 1,000 liters of air)	Surface Sample (per plate)
ISO 5 (PECs)	>1	>3
ISO 7 (buffer rooms and anteroom opening into a negative pressure room)	>10	>5
ISO 8 (anteroom opening only into positive pressure buffer rooms)	>100	>100

    M. Quality Control

        1. A policy needs to be established to describe the elements of control that support safe sterile compounding.

        2. The elements should be specific and measurable and identify the follow-up that would occur if excursions beyond stated limits occur.

V. Highlights of 2023 Revision of USP 797 Pharmaceutical Compounding—Sterile Preparations

Note: The 2023 revision of USP Chapter 797 becomes effective November 1, 2023, and it may be even longer before states adopt these changes into their regulations. This means it is unlikely you will see questions on these changes on the MPJE during 2023. The following summary is intended to highlight the upcoming changes to USP Chapter 797.

    A. Risk levels of sterile compounds previously listed in USP 797 have been eliminated and replaced with categories.

        1. Category 1 compounded sterile preparations (CSPs) can be prepared in a Segregated Compounding Area (CSP) and have a short beyond-use date (BUD) of 12 hours at room temperature or 24 hours refrigerated.

        2. Category 2 CSPs must be prepared in a cleanroom suite and may use the BUDs listed in Chapter 797, unless the stability of the compound requires a shorter time.

        3. Category 3 CSPs must be prepared in a cleanroom suite and may use extended BUDs as listed in Chapter 797 if all additional facility, personnel, testing, and monitoring are completed successfully.

    B. Compounding of sterile hazardous drugs must also follow requirements in USP Chapter 800—Hazardous Drugs: Handling in Healthcare Settings.

    C. Compounding of sterile radiopharmacuticals must also follow requirements in USP Chapter 825—Radiopharmceuticals: Preparation, Compounding, Dispensing, and Repackaging.

D. Administration of CSPs is out of the scope of Chapter 797.

E. Preparation following manufacturer's instructions (such as reconstituting an FDA-approved antibiotic injection) is out of the scope of Chapter 797, provided it is limited to a single patient and will not be stored. "Immediate Use" requirements apply in most cases.

F. A designated person is required to oversee compounding activities.

G. Personnel mixing Category 1 or 2 CSPs must successfully complete a media fill test, gloved fingertip testing, and a surface sample initially and every 6 months.

H. Personnel mixing Category 3 CSPs must successfully complete a media fill test, gloved fingertip testing, and a surface sample initially and every 3 months.

I. If a compounding aseptic isolator (CAI or CACI) is used, it must be in a cleanroom suite to use the full BUDs allowed by Chapter 797.

    1. If a CAI is not in a compounding suite, the requirements for a SCA must be met to use the BUDs allowed in a SCA.

    2. A CACI must be in the facility designs allowed in Chapter 800.

J. Environmental monitoring surface sampling must be completed monthly for Categories 1 and 2 . Category 3 has additional requirements.

K. Master Formulation Records and Compounding Records must be maintained.

VI. USP 800 Hazardous Drug—Compounding in Healthcare Settings
USP Chapter 800 became official on December 1, 2019, and will become "compendially applicable" (meaning, enforceable under federal regulations) on November 1, 2023. Some states and accreditation organizations expect compliance now; others will wait for the revisions of 795 and 797 to become official.

A. Introduction and Scope

    1. Chapter 800 details practice and quality standards for handling hazardous drugs (HDs) in various healthcare settings. The chapter discusses the handling of HDs from receipt to storage, compounding, dispensing, administration, and disposal of both nonsterile and sterile preparations. Included in the chapter is information on proper engineering controls and quality standards, personnel training, labeling, packaging, and transport and disposal of HDs, along with measures for spill control, documentation of all aspects of the handling of HDs, and medical surveillance.

2. Chapter 800 applies to all healthcare personnel and all entities who handle hazardous drugs. These personnel and entities include, but are not limited to, pharmacists, pharmacy technicians, pharmacies, physicians, nurses, hospital physician assistants, home healthcare workers, physician practice facilities, veterinarians, veterinary technicians, and veterinary hospitals and facilities. Entities that handle HDs must incorporate Chapter 800 standards into occupational safety standards.

3. The Occupational Safety and Health Administration (OSHA) includes hazardous drugs in their hazardous materials requirements, but does not include details of specific agents. Some states have additional state OSHA requirements.

B. List of Hazardous Drugs

1. The National Institute of Occupational Safety and Health (NIOSH) maintains a list of hazardous drugs (HDs) used in healthcare. This list is updated approximately every two years. Chapter 800 requires any entity that stores, compounds, prepares, transports, or administers hazardous drugs to maintain a list of HDs used in the entity and to review the list at least every 12 months and update whenever a new agent or dosage form is used. Newly marketed HDs or dosage forms should be reviewed against the entity's list.

STUDY TIP: The NIOSH list is split into tables. Table 1 includes antineoplastic drugs that must be handled with all containment and work practices listed in USP 800. Other drugs may be exempted by organizational policy in an assessment of risk if alternative strategies to protect personnel are identified and implemented.

2. The NIOSH list comprises drugs that are hazardous to healthcare workers. These are drugs that are carcinogens, genotoxins, teratogens, reproductive toxins, or cause organ toxicity at low doses. This is a different situation than hazardous materials defined by the Environmental Protection Agency (EPA), which are hazardous to the environment. A few hazardous drugs are listed on both lists.

3. Some dosage forms of drugs defined as hazardous drugs may not pose a substantial risk of direct occupational exposure to healthcare workers. However, particulate matter from tablets, capsules, and/or packaging materials could present an exposure risk if it contacts skin or mucous membranes. Facilities using hazardous drugs must perform an assessment of risk at least annually to determine if new or alternate containment strategies need to be employed to mitigate risks for exposure from HDs.

4. Unintentional exposures to hazardous drugs have been documented. These include transdermal and transmucosal absorption, injection, and ingestion. Containers of HDs have been shown to be contaminated upon arrival to their intended destination. Accidental exposure is also possible for individuals handling body fluids; deactivating, decontaminating, or disinfecting areas contaminated with HDs; and/or contacting HD residue on drug containers, work surfaces, etc.

C. Responsibilities of Personnel Handling Hazardous Drugs
1. The chapter requires that each entity have a designated person to be responsible for developing and implementing HD handling procedures. This individual must be properly trained and qualified to oversee entity compliance with the chapter and applicable state and federal laws and regulations and to ensure competency of all individuals who may come into contact with HDs.

2. All persons involved in the handling of HDs must have a fundamental understanding of practices and precautions and of the evaluation of procedures to ensure the safety and quality of the final HD product or preparation to minimize the risk of harm to the intended patient.

D. Facilities and Engineering Controls
1. At each stage of the handling of HDs there must be conditions and policies in place to promote safety for patients, workers, and the environment.
2. Signs must be placed at entrances to HD handling areas. Access to these areas of a facility should be limited only to properly trained and authorized personnel.
3. The chapter requires that there be designated areas for receiving and unpacking HDs, for storing HDs, and for compounding of nonsterile and sterile preparations.
4. Certain areas must have a negative pressure gradient with respect to surrounding areas of the facilities to reduce the risk of contaminating areas where non-HD-authorized individuals work. These negative pressure areas should have an uninterrupted power source in the event of a loss of power to the facility.

E. Receipt of HDs
1. According to Chapter 800, all HDs and all hazardous drug active pharmaceutical ingredients (HD-APIs) must be removed from shipping containers in an area that is negative pressure or neutral pressure relative to the surrounding areas. General receiving areas are acceptable as long as they are not positive pressure areas.
2. In addition, shipping cartons containing HDs and/or HD-APIs must not be opened in sterile compounding or positive pressure areas.

F. Storage of HDs
1. HDs must be stored in areas that can prevent or contain spillage or breakage of a container if it falls. However, HDs must not be stored on the floor.
2. Antineoplastic HDs in NIOSH Table 1 that will be compounded to make the final preparation, and Active Pharmaceutical Ingredient (API) of any NIOSH HDs, must be stored in an area away from non-HDs to prevent contamination or personnel exposure.

3. The room for storage of NIOSH Table 1 antineoplastic HDs that will be compounded and HD-APIs must be vented to the exterior of the facility and must have at least 12 air changes per hour (ACPH).

4. Final dosage forms of NIOSH Table 1 HDs and other HDs may be stored with non-HD drug inventory if permitted by entity policy in the Assessment of Risk.

G. Compounding with HDs

1. To help minimize the risk of exposure in a pharmacy compounding HDs, detailed standard operating procedures (SOPs) and training requirements must be developed. Workers must wear personal protective equipment (PPE) designed to be resistant to hazardous drugs. Goggles and face shields should be worn if splashing is possible, and respiratory protection should be worn if the HD is volatile or if particulate matter can become airborne.

2. Containment engineering controls to protect a preparation from microbial (if final preparation is to be sterile) and cross-contamination are required throughout the compounding procedures.

3. Containment engineering controls are divided into three types:
   a. Containment Primary Engineering Control (C-PEC);
   b. Containment Secondary Engineering Control (C-SEC); and
   c. Containment Supplemental Engineering Controls.

4. A C-PEC is a ventilated device designed to minimize the risk of exposure to the compounder and to the environment when HDs are handled directly. Containment Ventilated Enclosures (CVEs, often called powder containment hoods) are devices used only for nonsterile preparations. Biological Safety Cabinets (BSCs) and Compounding Aseptic Containment Isolators (CACIs) are used for sterile preparations and must maintain ISO 5 air cleanliness and have unidirectional air flow. The C-PEC must be operated continuously if used for sterile compounding or if it supplies some or all of the negative pressure for the room.

STUDY TIP: ISO class is determined by the number of particles larger than 0.5 microns in a volume of air. The smaller the ISO number, the cleaner the air. C-PECs must be ISO 5 or cleaner. Anterooms that open into a negative pressure room and buffer rooms must be ISO 7 or cleaner.

---

5. A C-SEC is the room in which the C-PEC is located. It can be a compounding suite (containing an anteroom and buffer room) or a containment segregated compounding area.
6. C-SECs must be used for compounding both nonsterile and sterile preparations and must:
   a. Be a room with fixed walls that is separate from non-hazardous storage or compounding;
   b. Have a negative pressure gradient of 0.010–0.030" with respect to adjacent areas;
   c. Have appropriate air exchange (ACPH); and
   d. Be vented to the exterior of the facility.

STUDY TIP: The separate room and negative pressure work to contain the hazard. External ventilation and air changes per hour work to remove the hazard.

---

7. Containment supplemental engineering controls, such as closed system drug-transfer devices (CSTDs), provide additional protection from exposure of the compounder to one or more HDs. CSTDs must be used for administration of Table 1 NIOSH antineoplastics and should be used for compounding.
8. An eyewash station and other applicable emergency safety equipment (e.g., safety showers, fire blankets, etc.) meeting applicable laws and regulations must be readily available, and a sink must be available for hand washing. However, all water sources and drains must be located outside the buffer room and at least one meter from the C-PEC or entrance to any negative pressure room.
9. For entities where compounding of both sterile and non-sterile HDs is performed, the C-PECs must be located in separate rooms, unless the C-PECs used for nonsterile compounding can effectively maintain ISO 7 air quality in the room. If the C-PECs for nonsterile and sterile compounding are located in the same room, they must be placed at least one meter apart. If the C-PECs are in the same room, any nonsterile compounding that generates particulate matter may not be performed when sterile compounding is being performed.
10. A professional certifier must assess the primary and secondary engineering controls every six months. The C-PECs and

C-SECs must meet the criteria listed in USP 797 (for facilities used for compounding sterile HDs) and USP 800 (for all facilities that compound HDs).

H. Nonsterile Compounding with HDs

1. In addition to following the regulations set forth in this chapter, entities involved in compounding nonsterile preparation, regardless of whether the compounding involves HDs or not, must also comply with the requirements of USP Chapter 795, Pharmaceutical Compounding—Nonsterile Preparations.

2. A C-PEC may not be required if the entity compounds only nonsterile, non-HD drugs, or if the entity is not manipulating HDs in any form except handling the final dosage forms (e.g., counting or repackaging tablets or capsules). This must be detailed in the Assessment of Risk.

3. C-PECs used only for nonsterile HD compounding are negative pressure devices but are not required to be ISO classified nor have unidirectional air flow.

Requirements for C-PECs and C-SECs for compounding nonsterile HDs are summarized in the following table:

ENGINEERING CONTROLS FOR NON-STERILE HD COMPOUNDING

C-PEC	C-SEC
Externally vented (preferred) or redundant-HEPA filtered with HEPA filters in series	Room separate from nonhazardous activities
	Negative pressure (0.010–0.030-inch water column) relative to adjacent areas
	Externally vented
	12 ACPH

I. Sterile Compounding with HDs

1. In addition to following the regulations set forth in this chapter, entities involved in compounding sterile preparation, regardless of whether the compounding involves HDs or not, must also comply with the requirements of USP Chapter 797, Pharmaceutical Compounding—Sterile Preparations.

2. All C-PECs used for the purpose of compounding sterile hazardous drugs must be vented to the outside.

3. As is the case with PECs used in the compounding of sterile non-HD preparations, C-PECs must maintain an ISO Class 5 or better air quality.

4. Laminar air flow workbenches or Compounding Aseptic Isolators (CAIs) are not acceptable for compounding antineoplastic HDs because they are positive pressure devices. Requirements for C-PECs and C-SECs for compounding sterile HDs are summarized in the following table:

ENGINEERING CONTROLS FOR STERILE HD COMPOUNDING

C-SEC Configuration	C-PEC Requirements	C-SEC Requirements
ISO Class 7 buffer room with ISO Class 7 anteroom	• Vented Externally • Examples: Class II BSC or CACI	• Room separate from non-hazardous activities • Vented Externally • 30 ACPH • Positive pressure anteroom • Negative pressure as described previously in buffer room
Unclassified C-SCA	• Vented Externally • Examples: Class II BSC or CACI	• Room separate from non-hazardous activities • Vented Externally • 12 ACPH • Negative pressure as described previously

J. Documentation and Standard Operating Procedures (SOPs)
  1. Any entity handling HDs must maintain SOPs for safe handling of HDs at all stages and locations where HDs are found in the facility.
  2. These SOPs are to be reviewed at least annually and should include a hazard communication program, occupational safety program, designation of HD areas, and items discussed above.
K. Receiving, Labeling, Packaging, Transport, and Disposal
  1. A facility must establish SOPs for the receiving, labeling, packaging, transport, and disposal of HDs.
  2. Transport of HDs must be labeled, stored, and handled in accordance with applicable federal, state, and local regulations.
  3. HDs must be transported in containers that minimize the risk of breakage and leakage.
L. Personnel Training
All personnel who handle HDs must be properly trained based on job function. The training must be documented.

M. Personal Protective Equipment
1. NIOSH documents provide guidance on personal protective equipment (PPE) such as not reusing disposable PPE and decontaminating reusable PPE.
2. Chapter 800 requires gowns, head and hair covers, shoe covers, and two pairs of powderless chemotherapy gloves when compounding either nonsterile or sterile antineoplastic agents. Two pairs of chemotherapy gloves and gowns resistant to permeability by HDs are also required when administering injectable antineoplastic HDs. One pair of chemo gloves must be worn when receiving NIOSH Table 1 antineoplastic HDs.
3. For other activities, the facility's SOPs must describe appropriate PPE to be worn. SOPs must be based on risk of exposure and activities.
4. At all stages of the handling of HDs, from receiving to waste disposal, PPE must be worn.
5. Chemotherapy gloves must meet the American Society of Testing Materials (ASTM) standard D6978 and should be worn when handling any HD. Chapter 800 states that chemotherapy gloves should be changed every 30 minutes unless the manufacturer recommends different intervals.
6. Chapter 800 states that gowns must close in the back, be disposable, and resist permeability of HDs. Gowns must be changed per the manufacturer's information for permeation of the gown. If there is no information from the manufacturer, then Chapter 800 states gowns are to be changed every 2–3 hours or immediately after a splash or spill. Personnel are not to wear in other areas of a facility the same gown that was worn in HD handling areas.
7. A second pair of shoe covers must be donned before entering the C-SEC and must be removed before leaving the HD handling areas and entering other areas of the facility.
8. Appropriate face and eye protection are to be worn when there is a risk of spills or splashes of HDs. Safety eyeglasses with side shields do not provide adequate protection.
9. When unpacking HDs not contained in plastic, personnel should wear elastomeric half-face masks which have been fit-tested with a P100 filter and a multi-gas cartridge.
10. All worn PPE should be considered contaminated and placed in an appropriate waste container to be disposed of properly.

PPE used in compounding HDs should be discarded in
proper containers before leaving the C-SEC.

N. Cleaning
1. The cleaning process for hazardous drugs must start with
deactivating the drug (when possible) and decontaminating
the surfaces that the HDs have touched.
2. After decontamination, the surfaces must be cleaned then
disinfected.

STUDY TIP: Few HDs have specific information concerning how to deactivate
them, so decontaminating the surfaces touched in the C-PEC and C-SEC is cru-
cial. Decontamination is done with a properly diluted oxidizer or other agent
intended to eliminate HDs. Cleaning is done with a properly diluted detergent.
Disinfection is done with isopropyl alcohol, which must be sterile for use in
C-PECs used for sterile compounding.

O. Spill Control
Facility policies must include the steps to take when a spill
occurs.
P. Medical Surveillance
1. As part of a comprehensive exposure control program, medical surveillance complements all other attempts by Chapter 800 to minimize risks to healthcare workers. Medical
surveillance is recommended but not required by USP 800.
2. Elements of an appropriate medical surveillance program
must be consistent with an entity's policies, and medical
records should be consistent with regulations set forth by the
Occupational Safety and Health Administration (OSHA).
3. Chapter 800 outlines elements of a medical surveillance
plan that should be included for all healthcare workers who
may come into contact with hazardous drugs. The chapter
also describes elements that should be included in a follow-
up plan should HD exposure-related health changes occur.
Again, the elements in the recommended medical surveillance and follow-up plans are not exhaustive, but they provide a good basis for the development of an appropriate program. Once again, however, any medical surveillance plan
should follow entity policies.
Q. Environmental Quality and Control
1. While there are no currently accepted limits for HD surface contamination, Chapter 800 states that surface wipe

sampling for HDs should be performed routinely to ensure that cleaning procedures are effective in removing remaining HD residues after handling or compounding.

2. Surface wipe sampling should include, but not necessarily be limited to, the inside surface of the C-PEC and any equipment contained in it, pass-through chambers, staging surfaces, areas adjacent to the C-PEC, areas immediately outside the buffer room or C-SEC, and patient administration areas.

3. The chapter continues by saying that if any measurable HD residue is found, the designated person should consider taking actions such as reevaluating work practices, retraining personnel, etc.

CHAPTER FIVE
Self-Assessment Questions

CHAPTER FIVE
Self-Assessment Questions

Important: All of these questions are based on federal law only, which, as explained earlier in the book, is not the best way to prepare for the MPJE because if a state law is stricter, the correct answer could be different. Also, many MPJE questions are based only on state law. Nevertheless, these questions should help you determine your level of understanding of the material in this book and your general knowledge of the most important federal laws and rules likely to appear on the MPJE. No representation is made that these questions are similar to questions on the actual MPJE. An answer key with explanations follows at the end of this section.

For more MPJE resources go to mpjereviews.com.

1. Pharmacist Bill orders and receives a bottle of generic glipizide from his supplier. Bill notices the label of the bottle is crooked and some of the lettering on the label appears to have different fonts in the same word. Bill calls the supplier to verify the transaction data and learns that the lot number on the bottle is not a valid lot number for that brand of glipizide. What is Bill required to do? **Select all that apply.**
   a. Notify FDA and all trading partners of this illegitimate product.
   b. Take steps to work with the manufacturer to prevent the illegitimate product from reaching patients.
   c. Order a Class I recall of the drug.
   d. Notify DEA.

2. Which of the following is not required on the label of an OTC product?
   a. Adequate directions for safe and effective use
   b. Name and address of the manufacturer, packager, or distributor
   c. Inactive ingredients
   d. Patient Package Insert

3. Fiorinal® is classified as
   a. A listed chemical
   b. A Schedule III controlled substance
   c. A Schedule IV controlled substance
   d. An exempt prescription product

4. When utilizing a DEA Form 222 to order Schedule II controlled substances, who is responsible for making a copy of the form?
   a. The supplier
   b. The purchaser
   c. The DEA
   d. The PDMP manager

5. The daily sales purchase limit for pseudoephedrine products is
   a. 0.6 g of base product
   b. 2.6 g of base product
   c. 3.6 g of base product
   d. 120 tablets

6. CMS requires that consultant pharmacists perform a medication regimen review for long-term care patients
   a. When requested by the facility
   b. At least weekly
   c. At least every 30 days
   d. When a medication error occurs

7. Dr. Costa calls your pharmacy and asks if she can call in a prescription for Vicodin for Mr. Garcia, a cancer patient who is well known to you. Dr. Costa states that Mr. Garcia cannot get relief from any other pain medication, and that Mr. Garcia is unable to get to her office to pick up a prescription. She asks if you can fill the prescription and deliver it to Mr. Garcia's house. Which of the following is true?
   a. You cannot take a verbal prescription for Vicodin under these circumstances because Mr. Garcia is not a hospice patient.
   b. You can take the verbal prescription, but Dr. Costa must send you a written or electronic prescription for the Vicodin within 7 days.
   c. You can take the verbal prescription and fill the prescription, but it can only be for a 72-hour supply.
   d. Both b and c

8. Which of the following drugs may be prescribed by a DATA-waived practitioner for treatment of narcotic addiction? **Select all that apply.**
   a. Buprenorphine
   b. A 3-day supply of any narcotic
   c. Buprenorphine/Naloxone combination
   d. Methadone

9. A fire broke out in the front part of Debra's pharmacy, but the flames did not reach the prescription department. Can the drugs still be dispensed?
   a. Yes, as long as the containers are all closed
   b. Yes, unless the drugs are heat sensitive
   c. Yes, but only after notifying patients that their prescription may have been exposed to smoke
   d. No, the smoke from the fire may have adulterated the drugs

10. Sterile preparations must be compounded in a primary engineering control device which is capable of maintaining at least
    a. ISO Class 3 conditions
    b. ISO Class 5 conditions
    c. ISO Class 7 conditions
    d. ISO Class 8 conditions

11. What must be provided prior to a patient picking up a refill of a birth control prescription?
    a. A safety data sheet
    b. A package insert
    c. A Patient Package Insert
    d. A Medication Guide

12. Anabolic steroids are classified under which schedule?
    a. Schedule II
    b. Schedule III
    c. Schedule IV
    d. Schedule V
    e. None of the above

13. A DEA Form 41 is used to document
   a. Transfer of controlled substances to another registrant
   b. Transfer of controlled substances to a Narcotic Treatment Facility
   c. Loss or theft of controlled substances
   d. Destruction of controlled substances
   e. None of the above

14. Which of the following OTC products is not required to be packaged in tamper-resistant packaging?
   a. Cepacol throat lozenges
   b. NyQuil liquid
   c. Zaditor eye drops
   d. Imodium caplets

15. A nursing home patient who is prescribed estrogen must receive a copy of the Patient Package Insert
   a. After one week of therapy
   b. Prior to the administration of the first dose and then every 30 days
   c. Annually
   d. If the doctor specifically requests it be given

16. For which class of recall is there a reasonable probability that the product could cause serious adverse effects or death?
   a. Class I
   b. Class II
   c. Class III
   d. Class IV

17. Dr. Galloway writes a prescription for Percocet on July 7, 2023. What is the last day the prescription can be dispensed?
   a. July 14, 2023
   b. July 28, 2023
   c. January 7, 2024
   d. Technically there is no expiration date, but the pharmacist should use professional judgment.

18. Place the following in order from the shortest time to the longest time.

   a. Time limit a supplier has to fill an order on a DEA 222 Form for fentanyl.

   b. Time limit for obtaining all authorized refills on a prescription for carisoprodol.

   c. Time limit for obtaining all partial fills of a prescription for methylphenidate if requested by the patient.

   d. Time limit for obtaining a written or electronic prescription after receiving an emergency verbal order for meperidine.

19. Which of the following is NOT a permissible use or disclosure of protected health information under HIPAA?

   a. Providing a list of all prescription medications to a patient's primary care physician

   b. Sending prescription information to a third-party insurance company for payment purposes

   c. Sending coupons for diapers to all pharmacy customers taking prenatal vitamins

   d. Providing a face-to-face recommendation of an OTC product to a patient based on the patient's symptoms and drug allergy profile

20. If a supplier cannot provide the entire quantity of a Schedule II controlled substance ordered on a DEA Form 222, the remaining quantity must be sent

   a. Within 72 hours

   b. Within 7 days

   c. Within 30 days

   d. Within 60 days

   e. None of the above

21. Which of the following products requires a prescription to be dispensed?

   a. Humalog®

   b. Humulin N®

   c. Lantus®

   d. Both a and c

22. Secobarbital in suppository form is classified under what schedule?
   a. Schedule II
   b. Schedule III
   c. Schedule IV
   d. Schedule V

23. Which of the following is not part of the transaction data required to be maintained by a pharmacy when it purchases most prescription drugs from a wholesaler or manufacturer?
   a. Transaction Information
   b. Transaction History
   c. Transaction Statement
   d. Transaction Certification

24. Under the iPLEDGE Risk Evaluation and Mitigation Strategy (REMS) for isotretinoin, the maximum quantity that can be dispensed is a
   a. 7-day supply
   b. 14-day supply
   c. 30-day supply
   d. 60-day supply

25. Which of the following is true regarding a Power of Attorney authorizing a person to order Schedule II controlled substances? **Select all that apply.**
   a. A copy of the Power of Attorney must be sent to DEA.
   b. It must be signed by two witnesses.
   c. The person receiving the authority is called the attorney-in-fact.
   d. The person receiving the authority must be a pharmacist.

26. Pharmacist Vincent has some expired morphine tablets he would like to send to a reverse distributor for destruction. What documentation is required to accomplish this?
   a. DEA Form 222
   b. DEA Form 41
   c. DEA Form 106
   d. An invoice

27. A nonprescription bottle of 1 and ¼ grain aspirin tablets cannot contain more than
    a. 24 tablets
    b. 36 tablets
    c. 50 tablets
    d. 100 tablets

28. A pharmacist received a bottle of generic tetracycline capsules from a wholesaler. The label stated that each capsule contained 500 mg of the drug when it only contained 250 mg of the drug. There was nothing about the drug that would indicate to the pharmacist that this problem existed. The pharmacist dispensed several prescriptions before the problem was detected. Which of the following statements is true regarding the tetracycline?
    a. It is adulterated only.
    b. It is misbranded only.
    c. It is neither adulterated nor misbranded but is instead a minor technical violation of the potency requirements.
    d. It is both adulterated and misbranded.
    e. It is in violation of the Poison Prevention Packaging Act.

29. Which of the following products is required to be dispensed with the warning: "Caution: Federal law prohibits the transfer of this drug to any person other than the patient for whom it was prescribed"?
    a. Buprenorphine
    b. Naloxone
    c. Robitussin AC
    d. Lipitor
    e. All of the above

30. Which of the following is likely to be outside the scope of practice for a dentist to prescribe?
    a. Alprazolam
    b. Amoxicillin
    c. Oral contraceptives
    d. Lidocaine gel

31. Dr. Smith sets up a new private practice near your pharmacy. Soon after, you begin to receive several prescriptions for methadone written by Dr. Smith. You call Dr. Smith and she explains to you that she is treating patients for opioid addiction. You should

    a. Document this conversation and continue to fill the methadone prescriptions.

    b. Ask Dr. Smith for her Drug Addiction Treatment Act (DATA) waiver identification code or "X" number and continue to fill the methadone prescriptions.

    c. Explain to Dr. Smith that she cannot prescribe methadone to treat opioid addiction, and that you must refuse to fill any further prescriptions for methadone from Dr. Smith.

    d. Fill prescriptions for methadone 10 mg from Dr. Smith but refuse to fill prescriptions for methadone 40 mg.

32. On September 3, 2023, Dr. Galloway issues three prescriptions to Sally for Adderall. Each prescription is for a 30-day supply. The prescriptions are each written on separate prescription forms and all are dated September 3, 2023. Prescription #1 contains no additional instructions. On Prescription #2, Dr. Galloway writes, "Do not fill before October 1, 2023." On prescription #3, Dr. Galloway writes, "Do not fill before November 1, 2023." Which of the following is true?

    a. Dr. Galloway cannot postdate Schedule II controlled substance prescriptions in this manner; therefore, Prescription #2 and Prescription #3 are not valid.

    b. All the prescriptions are valid and the earliest fill dates must be followed.

    c. None of the prescriptions are valid because Adderall cannot be prescribed on written prescriptions.

    d. None of the prescriptions are valid because Adderall can only be prescribed for a 10-day supply.

33. A pharmacist receives prescriptions for 12 different patients from the same physician over a 3-hour period. All of the prescriptions are written for patients from out of state and for the same combination of Vicodin, Xanax, and Soma. Which of the following are true? **Select all that apply.**

   a. If the pharmacist confirms that the physician has a valid license and DEA number, the prescriptions are likely valid and can be filled.

   b. If the pharmacist calls the physician and the physician confirms that he or she wrote the prescriptions and saw the patients, the prescriptions are likely valid and can be filled.

   c. The prescriptions are not likely to be valid because they appear to have not been issued for a legitimate medical purpose.

   d. If the pharmacist fills the prescriptions, he or she could be subject to disciplinary action by the state board of pharmacy.

34. Pharmacist Fred believes that customers would like to buy small quantities of nonprescription drugs, and decides to repackage bottles of 100 ibuprofen 200 mg tablets into amber prescription vials of 10 tablets and then sells them to the public. The vials are labeled with the name of the drug, the manufacturer, the lot number, and the expiration date from the original bottles. Which of the following statements are true? **Select all that apply.**

   a. Pharmacist Fred can repackage in this manner because it is for his own use in the pharmacy.

   b. Pharmacist Fred has misbranded the ibuprofen.

   c. The repackaging by Pharmacist Fred is considered compounding and within the practice of pharmacy.

   d. The repackaging by Pharmacist Fred is considered manufacturing.

35. For which of the following prescriptions can a fax serve as the original prescription?

   a. A prescription for Demerol tablets for a 30-year-old postal worker

   b. A prescription for Ritalin tablets for a 12-year-old boy who lives with his parents

   c. A prescription for methamphetamine tablets for a 78-year-old LTCF patient

   d. A prescription for a morphine injection for an 86-year-old hospice patient

   e. Both c and d

36. All partial dispensings of Schedule II controlled substances for a nursing home patient must be completed within
   a. 72 hours
   b. 7 days
   c. 30 days
   d. 60 days

37. What is the maximum number of individuals in a pharmacy that can be granted authority to sign a DEA Form 222 using a Power of Attorney?
   a. 3 persons total
   b. 3 persons in a community pharmacy, but no limit in a hospital pharmacy
   c. 3 persons total, but only one may be a pharmacy technician
   d. There is no maximum number

38. Which of the following is true regarding a pharmacy that is an Authorized Collector?
   a. The inner liner of a collection receptacle must be removed by or under the supervision of at least two employees of the pharmacy.
   b. The inner liner of a collection receptacle may not be removed by employees of the pharmacy.
   c. The contents in a collection receptacle must be inventoried before being destroyed or being sent for destruction.
   d. Collection receptacles may be placed anywhere within the pharmacy.

39. Paula Pharmacist recently attended the American Pharmacists Association Annual Meeting and attended three continuing education programs. Each program was two hours in length and was accredited by the Accreditation Council for Pharmacy Education (ACPE). How many continuing education units (CEUs) did Paula earn?
   a. 3
   b. 0.3
   c. 6
   d. 0.6

40. Which OTC product label must contain a warning about liver toxicity?
    a. Nonsteroidal Anti-Inflammatory Drugs (NSAIDs)
    b. Phenacetin
    c. Acetaminophen
    d. Ipecac Syrup

41. FDA has approved a new drug, Pevisar, but requires patients to have documented proof of a normal enzyme test before the drug can be dispensed and every 6 months thereafter. Such a requirement is part of:
    a. A Risk Evaluation and Mitigation Strategy
    b. A Risk Management Program
    c. A Continuous Quality Improvement Program
    d. Elements for Safe Dispensing

42. MTC, a medical device manufacturer, has developed a new medical device for monitoring blood glucose levels in diabetic patients. MTC would like to have this device reimbursed through patients' prescription drug benefits, so they included an NDC number on the product's label. Which of the following statements are true? **Select all that apply.**
    a. Since an NDC number is not technically required, MTC is able to do this, but for reimbursement purposes only.
    b. If MTC places the NDC number on the label, they cannot include a Unique Device Identifier.
    c. MTC is required to have a Unique Device Identifier on the product's label.
    d. Placing an NDC number on the label would make the product misbranded.

43. Which of the following may be in possession of prescription drug samples? **Select all that apply.**
    a. A hospital pharmacy that has been requested to maintain samples by a physician associated with the hospital
    b. A physician assistant who has prescriptive authority in a state
    c. A community pharmacy located in a medical office building that has been requested to maintain samples by the physicians located in the same building
    d. A mail-service pharmacy

44. An outsourcing facility must report serious adverse effects related to any drug they produce within
   a. 3 days
   b. 10 days
   c. 15 days
   d. 20 days

45. Which of the following products are exempt from the requirements of the Poison Prevention Packaging Act? **Select all that apply.**
   a. Isosorbide dinitrate 2.5 mg chewable tablets
   b. Nitroglycerin 2.5 mg extended release capsules
   c. Isosorbide dinitrate 10 mg tablets
   d. Nitrostat 0.4 mg sublingual tablets

46. Which of the following is true regarding refill reminder programs?
   a. Since the purpose of these programs is to encourage the sale of future prescriptions, they are considered marketing programs and require a HIPAA authorization from the patient.
   b. If the refill reminder program is for prescription drugs currently prescribed for a patient, they are considered treatment and do not require a HIPAA authorization from the patient.
   c. Refill reminders may not be sent via text message.
   d. Refill reminders are not allowed for controlled substances.

47. You receive a prescription calling for you to compound and dispense a one-pint bottle of a solution containing 120 mg of acetaminophen and 16 mg of codeine per teaspoon mixed with cherry flavoring. What schedule would this product be in?
   a. Schedule II
   b. Schedule III
   c. Schedule IV
   d. Schedule V

48. DEA registrations beginning with the letter M are issued to
   a. Medical Doctors (M.D.s)
   b. Medical Clinics
   c. Mobile Narcotic Treatment Centers
   d. Physician Assistants

49. You work in a community pharmacy across the street from a large teaching hospital. You receive a prescription for Percocet written for a 12-year-old child who was seen in the emergency room of the hospital. The prescription is written by Dr. Anh, an internal medicine resident at the hospital, on a hospital prescription pad and has the hospital's DEA number followed by "A16." Which of the following is true?

    a. A prescription for Percocet for a 12-year-old child cannot be dispensed.

    b. The prescription is valid but may only be dispensed by the hospital's outpatient pharmacy.

    c. The A16 is an indication that only a quantity of 16 may be dispensed.

    d. The prescription may be filled at your pharmacy.

50. CSOS Signing Certificates are issued to

    a. The pharmacy holding the DEA registration

    b. The pharmacist-in-charge

    c. The DEA registrant (owner) or person who has Power of Attorney

    d. The head of IT security at a pharmacy

51. DEA Form 41 would be used to document which of the following? **Select all that apply.**

    a. Destruction of expired Demerol tablets in a hospital pharmacy

    b. Wasting of a partial quantity of a morphine 10 mg ampule in a hospital

    c. Destruction of controlled substances from a collection receptacle by a pharmacy that is an authorized collector

    d. Sending an expired bottle of tramadol to a reverse distributor

52. Which of the following is true regarding DEA Form 106?

    a. It should be used to document waste of a controlled substance.

    b. It must be signed by two witnesses.

    c. It must be sent to DEA within one business day of discovery of a significant loss or theft of controlled substances.

    d. It must be used to report any theft of a controlled substance.

53. The maximum number of patients that can be treated by a DATA-waived physician is
   a. 30
   b. 100
   c. 275
   d. 300

54. USP General Chapters are examples of which type of documents?
   a. Goals
   b. Guidelines
   c. Standards
   d. Regulations

55. Pharmacist Pat is compounding eye drops from conventionally manufactured cefazolin injection and artificial tears. Which USP Chapter applies when compounding this preparation?
   a. USP 795
   b. USP 797
   c. USP 800
   d. USP 825

56. Compounding sterile antineoplastic agents must comply with which of the following USP Chapters?
   a. USP 795 and 1161
   b. USP 795 and 800
   c. USP 797 and 800
   d. USP 797 and 1161

57. Pharmacist Kurt reconstitutes a pharmacy bulk package of vancomycin to make a batch of 10 IV bags for dispensing today. What is the risk level of the batch of preparations he is compounding?
   a. Immediate Use
   b. Low Risk
   c. Medium Risk
   d. High Risk

58. Main Street Hospital Pharmacy has three areas where IVs are mixed: a suite in the main pharmacy consisting of an anteroom and a positive pressure buffer room where nonhazardous sterile preparations are mixed, a suite in the oncology unit with an anteroom and a negative pressure buffer room where hazardous sterile preparations are mixed, and a segregated compounding area (SCA) in the Surgical Services pharmacy satellite. Which areas need to be ISO 7?

    a. Anteroom in the main pharmacy and anteroom in the oncology unit

    b. Negative pressure buffer room and segregated compounding area

    c. Positive pressure buffer room and negative pressure buffer room

    d. Anteroom in the main pharmacy and negative pressure buffer room

59. Pharmacist Kevin is preparing the Assessment of Risk required by USP 800 to identify the hazards and mitigating strategies for his health system. Which organization maintains the list of drugs that are hazardous to healthcare personnel?

    a. National Association of Boards of Pharmacy

    b. American Pharmacists Association

    c. Occupational Safety and Health Administration

    d. National Institute of Occupational Safety and Health

60. Pharmacist Mary Ann is preparing a nonsterile compound that has been mixed before in her pharmacy. Which document should she refer to for the complete information to prepare the compound?

    a. Package Insert

    b. Master Formulation Record

    c. Compounding Record

    d. Safety Data Sheet

EXPLANATORY ANSWERS

For more MPJE resources go to mpjereviews.com.

1. A. and B.
This product is illegitimate under the Drug Supply Chain Security Act (DSCSA). Both A. and B. are obligations of a pharmacy under the DSCSA once an illegitimate product is identified. C. is incorrect because, although a recall may be initiated, that is not the obligation of the pharmacy. D. is incorrect because the DSCSA is enforced by FDA, not DEA.

2. D.
A Patient Package Insert is required for oral contraceptives and estrogen products, not OTC products.

3. B.
Fiorinal® (butalbital, aspirin, and caffeine) is a Schedule III controlled substance, but Fioricet® (butalbital, acetaminophen, caffeine) is an exempt product and is not a controlled substance under federal law.

4. B.
The original DEA Form 222 must be sent to the supplier, so the purchaser has to make a copy for their records before placing the order. This is required to be able to document the controlled substances that are received on the copy.

5. C.
Under the Combat Methamphetamine Epidemic Act, the daily sales limit for pseudoephedrine base product is 3.6 grams per day.

6. C.
CMS requires a consultant pharmacist to perform a medication regimen review every 30 days and must report any irregularities to the attending physician, the facility's medical director, and the facility's director of nursing.

7. B.
This qualifies as an emergency situation where a pharmacist can take a verbal order for a Schedule II drug. One of the requirements to do this is the prescriber must send an electronic or written prescription for the Schedule II drug within 7 days. There is not a requirement that the patient be in hospice. Under federal law, the amount that can be dispensed under an emergency verbal order for a Schedule II drug is the amount necessary to treat the patient during the emergency. It is not necessarily a 72-hour supply, although some states do specify a specific days' supply.

8. A. and C.
A DATA-waived practitioner can only prescribe two drugs to treat narcotic addiction: buprenorphine and buprenorphine/naloxone combination. While they may be able to prescribe other narcotics, including methadone for pain control, no prescriber may prescribe those products to treat narcotic addiction.

9. D.
Remember that a drug can be adulterated, even if the container it was in is sealed, if it has been held under conditions where it may have been contaminated. The fact that the product was exposed to excessive heat and/or smoke is enough to make the product adulterated.

10. B.
Primary engineering control (PEC) devices must be capable of maintaining ISO Class 5 air quality. You should also be familiar with ISO Class requirements for anterooms and buffer rooms.

11. C.
A Patient Package Insert is required to be provided to patients prescribed estrogens or oral contraceptives, including for refills. Do not get mixed up between a package insert, a Patient Package Insert, and a Medication Guide.

12. B.
Anabolic steroids are Schedule III controlled substances. Some states add additional products such as human growth hormone (HGH) and human chorionic gonadotropin (HCG) as controlled substances, although they are not scheduled under federal law.

13. D.

DEA Form 41 is for documenting destruction of controlled substances. Transfers of controlled substances require either an invoice for Schedule III–V products or a DEA Form 222 for Schedule II products. The theft or significant loss of controlled substances is documented on a DEA Form 106.

14. A.

Most OTC drugs are required to be packaged in tamper-evident packaging. Exceptions exist for dermatologicals, dentifrices, insulin products, and lozenges.

15. B.

Institutionalized patients, including nursing home and hospitalized patients, prescribed an estrogen or oral contraceptive are supposed to be given a Patient Package Insert prior to receiving the first dose and every 30 days thereafter. This is one of those things that does not happen in practice very often but is technically required under federal rules.

16. A.

Class I recalls are the most serious recalls, those where there is a reasonable probability of serious adverse effects or death.

17. D.

There is no expiration date on a single Schedule II prescription under federal law. This is just an anomaly in the federal law. Most states do have a time limit or expiration date for Schedule II prescriptions, so this is likely not the correct answer under most state laws. Be sure to check the rules in your state.

18. D.—Time limit for obtaining a written or electronic prescription after receiving an emergency verbal order for meperidine = 7 days
C.—Time limit for obtaining all partial fills of a prescription for methylphenidate if requested by the patient = 30 days
A.—Time limit a supplier has to fill an order on a DEA 222 Form for fentanyl = 60 days
B.—Time limit for obtaining all authorized refills on a prescription for carisoprodol = 6 months

19. C.

Sending diaper coupons to patients taking prenatal vitamins would be considered marketing because you are using the patients' protected health information (i.e., the fact that they are taking prenatal vitamins) to try to sell them a product, diapers. Sending a physician a list of a patient's medications fits within the treatment definition under HIPAA and does not require a patient's consent. Sending information to a third-party insurance plan is part of payment. Although recommending an OTC drug product sounds like it could be considered marketing, HIPAA has a specific exemption that allows this.

20. D.

A supplier has up to 60 days to fill an order of a Schedule II drug ordered on a DEA 222 Form.

21. D.

Both Lantus® and Humalog® are brands of insulin that require a prescription. Be sure to know those that require a prescription and those that do not.

22. B.

Secobarbital in suppository form is Schedule III, but in other dosage forms is Schedule II.

23. D.

Under the DSCSA, Transaction Data that must be provided for each purchase of a drug includes a transaction history, transaction statement, and transaction information. It does not include a transaction certification.

24. C.

The iPLEDGE Risk Evaluation and Mitigation Strategy (REMS) for isotretinoin is one of the most common REMS, and you should know the details of this program, including the limitation of a 30-day supply.

25. B. and C.

A registrant may authorize other individuals to sign DEA Form 222 to order Schedule II controlled substances by executing a Power of Attorney (POA). The person receiving the authority does not have to be a pharmacist. The POA must be signed by the person granting the authority (the registrant), the person receiving the authority (the attorney-in-fact), and two witnesses. The POA should be maintained in the pharmacy. It does not have to be sent to DEA.

26. A.
This is a transfer from one DEA registrant (the pharmacy) to another DEA registrant (the reverse distributor). Since morphine is a Schedule II drug, all transfers of Schedule II drugs must be made using a DEA Form 222. A DEA Form 41 is not used because the pharmacy is not destroying the drug. An invoice would be the correct answer if the drug involved were a Schedule III–V product.

27. B.
This is from those sets of federal regulations that apply to certain OTC products that include special labeling requirements. Within those rules are special requirements for pediatric (1 and ¼ grain) aspirin tablets that restrict sales to bottles of no more than 36 tablets. It also requires a warning regarding Reye's syndrome.

28. D.
Remember that when the label states something that is false or misleading, the product is misbranded. Here, the product lists one strength but inside the bottle is a different strength, so the product is misbranded. However, because this involves the strength of the product, it is also adulterated because the definition of adulteration includes when the drug's quality or strength falls below that which it represents.

29. A.
This is one of those tricky questions because most pharmacies put this warning on every prescription label, but it is only required for Schedule II–IV controlled substances. The only Schedule II–IV drug listed is buprenorphine. It is not required for Schedule V products under federal law because some Schedule V products may be sold without a prescription, so it would not make sense on those.

30. C.
A dentist can only prescribe drugs that are related to the practice of dentistry, and it is not likely that would include prescribing oral contraceptives.

31. C.

While methadone can be used to treat opioid addiction, it cannot be prescribed by a practitioner or dispensed by a pharmacy for this purpose. It can only be provided at a narcotic treatment center, and a pharmacy is not registered as a narcotic treatment center. A DATA-waived practitioner also cannot prescribe methadone for the treatment of opioid addiction. They can only prescribe buprenorphine and buprenorphine/naloxone combination. Do not get narcotic treatment centers confused with DATA-waived practitioners.

32. B.

The issuance of multiple Schedule II prescriptions on the same date is permitted by DEA if the subsequent prescriptions indicate the earliest fill date and the total quantity prescribed does not exceed a 90-day supply. In some states, Schedule II prescriptions may be required to be issued electronically, so written prescriptions may not be valid, but there is no such requirement under federal law, so that answer is not correct under federal law. There is also no federal law that restricts the quantity of a Schedule II prescription to a 10-day supply.

33. C. and D.

This is a clear example of a situation which requires a pharmacist to exercise their corresponding responsibility to ensure that controlled substance prescriptions are being issued for a legitimate medical purpose and in the usual course of professional practice. Simply relying on the fact that the prescriber has a valid DEA number, or even calling the prescriber to confirm that the patients were seen, is not enough to clear the numerous "red flags" in this situation. The prescriptions are not valid, and a pharmacist could face disciplinary action if he or she fills these prescriptions.

34. B. and D.

The repackaging of drug products, including OTC products, is considered manufacturing by FDA. The products would be misbranded because they do not contain all the required information on the label of an OTC product as required by FDA. While FDA does recognize some exceptions that allow pharmacists to prepackage drugs for their own use, such as packaging into unit-dose or compliance packaging, it does not include the repackaging of OTC products that are sold to the public.

35. E.

DEA requires Schedule II prescriptions to be written or electronic. Fax prescriptions are generally treated like verbal prescriptions and are not valid for Schedule II drugs. However, DEA recognizes a few exceptions to this rule, which include any Schedule II drug for patients in long-term care facilities and Schedule II narcotics for patients in hospice. Neither of the prescriptions for Demerol tablets or Ritalin tablets meet the exceptions.

36. D.

The time limit for obtaining all partial fills of Schedule II prescriptions depends on a few factors. If the pharmacist is unable to dispense the full quantity, then the remaining amount must be dispensed within 72 hours. If the patient or prescriber requests a partial fill, the remaining quantity must be dispensed within 30 days. If the patient is in a long-term care facility or has a terminal illness, the remaining quantity must be dispensed within 60 days. Remember, these are not refills.

37. D.

There is no limit to the number of people who can be given the authority to sign DEA Form 222 to order Schedule II controlled substances using a Power of Attorney. There is also no requirement that the person granted the authority must be a pharmacist.

38. A.

The inner liner of a collection receptacle for drugs must be removed by or under the supervision of at least two employees of the pharmacy. The drugs placed into a collection receptacle should not be inventoried, counted, handled, or removed by anyone at the pharmacy. Collection receptacles must be in the immediate proximity of the pharmacy department. They cannot be placed anywhere.

39. D.

It is a simple thing, but do not forget that the American Council for Pharmaceutical Education (ACPE) uses continuing education units (CEUs) rather than hours to accredit pharmacist continuing education programs, and a one-hour program is considered 0.1 CEU. In this case the 3 courses total 6 hours, or 0.6 CEUs.

40. C.

See Chapter 2 on special warning requirements for OTC drugs.

41. A.

Programs that require patients, doctors, or pharmacists to meet certain criteria, or have completed specific tasks before a drug can be prescribed or dispensed such as this, are required by FDA to manage a known or potential serious risk associated with a drug. These programs are called Risk Evaluation and Mitigation Strategies, or REMS. Part of a REM may be Elements to Assure Safe Use, not Elements to Assure Safe Dispensing.

42. C. and D.

Because it is a medical device, a Unique Device Identifier is required on the label. The National Drug Code (NDC) number may only be placed on drugs. Placing an NDC number on a medical device would cause that product to be misbranded.

43. A. and B.

Under the Prescription Drug Marketing Act, pharmacies are prohibited from having samples of prescription drugs. There is an exception for hospital pharmacies that are storing prescription drug samples on behalf of physicians affiliated with the hospital. Just having a pharmacy in a medical office building does not qualify for this exception. If a prescriber such as a physician assistant has the authority to prescribe prescription drugs in a state, he or she can also request and store prescription drug samples.

44. C.

Outsourcing facilities must report serious adverse effects to FDA for any drug they produce within 15 days. *See discussion on outsourcing facilities in Chapter 1.*

45. A. and D.

This question points out that you must know the details of the exemptions under the Poison Prevention Packaging Act, as even the same products may not be exempt depending on the strength and/or dosage form.

46. B.

HIPAA allows refill reminders for drugs a patient is currently taking or was taking in the last 90 days. This falls under the treatment exception under HIPAA, so it is not considered marketing. There is no federal restriction regarding refill reminders for controlled substances, but some state laws may have such a restriction.

47. B.

Always check to be sure the narcotic substance, codeine in this question, is being compounded with another therapeutic ingredient first because, if it is not, the answer will be Schedule II, regardless of the concentration. In this case, the codeine is being compounded with acetaminophen, so you do need to calculate the concentration of codeine: 16mg/5ml (teaspoon) = 320mg/100ml. This is greater than the maximum concentration for Schedule V of 200mg/ml and less than the maximum concentration for Schedule III of 1.8g/100ml, so this is a Schedule III prescription.

48. D.

The M in the first part of a DEA registration stands for "mid-level practitioner," and a physician assistant is a type of mid-level practitioner.

49. D.

An intern or resident in a hospital can issue controlled substance prescriptions using the hospital's DEA registration as long as it is for a patient that was treated at the hospital and the hospital uses a code or suffix on the DEA number to identify who the prescriber is. That is the A16 in this question. These prescriptions are valid and can be dispensed by any pharmacy, not just the hospital outpatient pharmacy.

50. C.

CSOS Signing Certificates are not assigned to the pharmacy, they are assigned to individuals. They can only be issued to the registrant, which in the case of a pharmacy would be the owner if it is a sole proprietor, a partner if it is a partnership, or a corporate officer if it is a corporation. They can also be issued to any individual who has a Power of Attorney to order a Schedule II controlled substance.

51. A. and C.

The DEA Form 41 is used to document the destruction of a controlled substance on the premises, but it is also used to document the destruction of a controlled substance from a collection receptacle if a pharmacy is an Authorized Collector. It is not used to document a transfer to a reverse distributor or for wasting a partial quantity.

52. D.

The DEA Form 106 is used to document a theft or significant loss of controlled substances. While an initial notice to the DEA must be made in writing within one business day of discovery, this does not mean the DEA 106 has to be completed by then. A pharmacy may need time to investigate the extent and scope of the theft or loss because the DEA Form 106 requires listing each controlled substance that was lost or stolen, and that may take some time. No witnesses are required to sign the DEA Form 106.

53. C.

A DATA-waived physician may be authorized to treat 30, 100, or 275 patients, but the maximum is 275.

54. C.

USP General Chapters are standards which are adopted by regulators, accreditation organizations, and professional societies.

55. B.

Ophthalmics—including drops—need to be sterile, so USP 797 applies. Cefazolin is not a hazardous drug, so USP 800 does not apply in this case.

56. C.

Compounding sterile hazardous drugs must comply with both USP 797 and 800.

57. C.

A pharmacy bulk package is a conventionally manufactured dosage form. Any batch from all sterile components is a medium risk preparation.

58. C.
Areas that must be ISO 7 or cleaner are buffer rooms (both positive and negative pressure) and anterooms that open into a negative pressure room. Anterooms that open only into positive pressure buffer rooms must be at least ISO 8. Segregated compounding areas do not need to be ISO classified.

59. D.
NIOSH is the organization that maintains the list of drugs that are hazardous to healthcare professionals.

60. B.
USP 795 requires a Master Formulation Record to be created for each nonsterile compound. It is the recipe to be used and includes components, amounts, equipment, technique, BUD assignment, and other elements to be able to replicate a compound.